THE STRUGGLE FOR RELIGIOUS
FREEDOM IN VIRGINIA:

THE BAPTISTS

Series XVIII   Nos. 10-11-12

JOHNS HOPKINS UNIVERSITY STUDIES

IN

HISTORICAL AND POLITICAL SCIENCE

HERBERT B. ADAMS, Editor

History is past Politics and Politics are present History.—*Freeman*

THE STRUGGLE FOR RELIGIOUS FREEDOM IN VIRGINIA:

THE BAPTISTS

By WILLIAM TAYLOR THOM

BALTIMORE
THE JOHNS HOPKINS PRESS
OCTOBER–NOVEMBER–DECEMBER, 1900

𝕿𝖍𝖊 𝕷𝖔𝖗𝖉 𝕭𝖆𝖑𝖙𝖎𝖒𝖔𝖗𝖊 𝕻𝖗𝖊𝖘𝖘
THE FRIEDENWALD COMPANY
BALTIMORE, MD., U. S. A.

CONTENTS

PREFACE

The aim kept steadily in view in the following pages is to set forth in all good faith the part played by the Baptists in bringing about Religious Freedom in Virginia; not to give a history of the Baptists themselves. That has been done only in so far as seemed needful to make plain the causes of their sudden rise and the sources of their influence among the people. The description of their political method is, I hope, clear; but that description would have been much more accurate and elaborate, as I believe, had some of the original manuscripts still in existence been accessible. The original petitions now slowly yielding to the tooth of time in the archives of the Virginia State Library would, through the signatures attached to them, have thrown great light upon the political conditions of the counties whence they came, as well as upon the membership of those General Assemblies to which they were addressed and of those which came immediately after. These manuscripts should have been published long ago.

It is hardly probable that I have reached all material now accessible, and I shall be glad of information throwing further light upon the subject; particularly so as I hope hereafter to make yet more plain what was accomplished by the Baptists in comparison with the action of the other denominations in the same struggle for freedom in religious matters.

My work on this subject was practically done before I became aware that the "Documentary History of the Struggle for Religious Freedom in Virginia," by Rev. C. F. James, was appearing in the columns of the *Religious Herald,* and before I could lay my hands on the edition of

Semple's *History,* by Rev. G. W. Beale, whom I hasten to thank for valuable aid in the preparation of the map prefixed to this sketch. I beg to make my acknowledgments also to Prof. H. B. Adams, Dr. J. C. Ballagh, and Mr. T. R. Ball, of the Johns Hopkins University; Prof. C. L. Cocke, of Hollins Institute, Virginia; Dr. J. L. M. Curry, of Washington, D. C.; Hon. A. R. Spofford, and Mr. Hugh Morrison, of the Library of Congress, and Mr. W. W. Scott, of the State Library of Virginia, for aid and courtesies most opportunely extended.

The map illustrating the growth of the Baptists between 1770 and 1776 is distinctly a trial map and does not lay claim to final accuracy. I have reproduced the crude outlines of the old Lewis map in the hope of impressing upon my readers the difference between the Virginia of the Revolutionary times and the Virginia of to-day. In spite of the help of Dr. Beale, I do not feel at all sure that the location of some of the churches is not wrong by many miles. Some of the churches, too, were not actually constituted until after 1776, but they were in process of formation and had their political effect before the end of that year.

Were it the custom of these "Studies," I should have asked permission to dedicate this sketch to my good friends, Professor Charles L. Cocke, Superintendent of Hollins Institute, Virginia, and Dr. J. L. M. Curry, Secretary of the Peabody and Slater Funds, with both of whom it has been my pleasant lot to work in the great field of school instruction, and who, through long and honored lives, have illustrated, the one as the foremost champion of female education in the South, the other as statesman, educator, and the dispenser of a vast educational charity, the highest type of noble Baptist manhood.

1899.   Wm. Taylor Thom.

THE STRUGGLE FOR RELIGIOUS FREE-
DOM IN VIRGINIA : THE BAPTISTS

I recollect with satisfaction that the religious society of which you are members have been, throughout America, uniformly and almost unanimously, the firm friends to civil liberty, and the persevering promoters of our glorious revolution.— George Washington's Letter of 1789.

The struggle for Religious Freedom in Virginia was really a part of that greater struggle for political freedom with which it was so nearly coincident in time. Much the same causes led to each; the logic of both was the same; and there was no time at which the religious struggle was not largely political and not clearly seen to be so by the leaders of thought. The struggle for independence was against external coercion; the struggle for religious freedom was against that external coercion as represented within the colony itself. The failure of the struggle for independence meant the failure of the struggle for religious freedom; but the achievement of independence did not necessarily mean the attainment of religious freedom. Hence the religious struggle outlasted the political, and hence also it assumed towards the end a vindictiveness not pleasant to contemplate.

Religious toleration had been attained some years before the Revolution drew near; and for that, credit is due chiefly to the Presbyterian population of the colony, as Dr. McIlwaine has shown in his account of the " Struggle for

Religious Toleration in Virginia."[1] Other elements of the population became actively involved as the dissatisfaction among the colonists hardened into resistance against the mother country; and among these elements, active in bringing about religious freedom, no one perhaps was of greater importance than the Baptists, with whom we have to do in the following pages.

When the struggle for religious toleration practically ceased with the French and Indian War and the "Parsons' Cause" in 1763, the Baptists were not of sufficient consequence to be even noticed by the historian. Eleven years later they are preparing to petition the legislature for the abolition of the Established Church. Evidently we must know something of them, must know who and whence they were, as a preliminary to understanding what they helped to bring about.

The accepted version, for the matter is disputed somewhat, seems to be that Baptists first came into Virginia about the year 1714 as English emigrants; that they settled in the southeastern part of the colony; and that they remained there practically unnoticed until they were taken up in the movement of which we are going to speak. After various vicissitudes, they still had a church at Pungo in Princess Anne county in 1762, but they had not influenced the life of the colony. They were known, it seems, as "General" Baptists.

About the year 1743 another party of Baptists came from Maryland into the lower Valley and settled at Mill Creek on the Opeckon in Berkeley county. About a dozen years later, in consequence of inroads of the Indians, a part of this congregation and their minister, John Garrard, probably a Pennsylvanian, removed across the Blue Ridge and settled on Ketocton Creek in Loudoun county, organizing

---

[1] Cf. H. R. McIlwaine, Religious Toleration in Virginia, Johns Hopkins University Studies in Historical and Political Science, 1894.

themselves into a church about 1755-56. A few years later, David Thomas, from Pennsylvania, a man of vigorous mind and, we are told, of a classical education, settled at Broad Run in Fauquier county, where a church was constituted and he was chosen pastor, probably in 1761. Thomas and Garrard travelled and preached extensively in this piedmont country. In 1770 these Baptists were spread through the Northern Neck of Virginia above Fredericksburg in the counties of Stafford, Fauquier, and Loudoun, and they had churches at that time at Mill Creek, in Berkeley county; at Smith's Creek in Shenandoah county; at Ketocton, New Valley, and Little River, in Loudoun county; at Broad Run, in Fauquier county; at Chappawamsic and Potomac Creek, in Stafford county; at Mountain Run, in Orange county; at Birch Creek, in Halifax county; with a membership, all told, of six hundred and twenty-four.[2]

These were known as the "Regular" Baptists; and although they were from time to time hindered by mobs and reprimanded by magistrates, they were not seriously interfered with. "The reason why the Regular Baptists were not so much persecuted as the Separates," says Semple, "was that they had, at an early date, applied to the General Court, and obtained licenses for particular places, under the toleration law of England; but few of their enemies knew the extent of these licenses; most supposing that they were, by them, authorized to preach anywhere in the county. One other reason for their moderate persecution perhaps was that the Regulars were not thought so enthusiastic as the Separates; and having Mr. Thomàs, a learned man, in their Society, they appeared much more respectable in the eyes of the enemies of truth."[3]   It is important

---

[2] Fristoe, Ketocton Association, pp. 5-10; Semple, 288; cf. also Semple, 43, 49, 141, 169, 174, 194, 290.

[3] The title of Thomas's little book is worthy of transcription in this connection:

"The Virginian Baptist: or a View and Defence of the Christo note this two-fold statement, that the Regular Baptists took out licenses from the General Court in due form of law, and that the presence of David Thomas as an educated man in their midst was of weight in protecting them against their neighbors.

The great Baptist influence in Virginia was that of the "Separate" Baptists, as they were called. They came into Virginia from North Carolina in the following way:

In 1754, Shubal Stearns, a native of Boston, who had become a Separate Baptist preacher in 1751, came south with a small party of New Englanders, called of the Spirit, as he conceived, to a great work. They halted first at Opeckon in Berkeley county, Virginia. Here he met his brother-in-law, Daniel Marshall, formerly a Presbyterian, now a Baptist preacher, who was just returned from a mission among the Indians. After a short stay in this part of the country, they moved on south to Guilford county, North Carolina, and, establishing themselves on Sandy Creek, founded a church which soon swelled from 16 to 606 members.[4]

Daniel Marshall made visits into Virginia, preaching and baptizing converts. "Among them was Dutton Lane (originally from near Baltimore, Maryland), who, shortly after his baptism, began to preach; a revival succeeded,

---

tian Religion, as it is professed by the Baptists of Virginia. In three Parts. Containing a true and faithful Account (1) Of their Principles, (2) Of their Orders as a Church, (3) Of the principal Objections made against them, especially in this Colony. With a serious Answer to each of them.

By David Thomas, A. M., and Baptist Minister of Fauquier, in Virginia.

Non haec tibi nunciat Auctor Ambiguus: Non ista vagis rumoribus. Ipse ego tibi. *Ovid Met.*

And thou Son of Man, show the House to the House of Israel, and let them measure the Pattern. Ezek. xliii., 10, 11.

Baltimore:

Printed by Enoch Story, living in Gay Street. MDCCLXXIV."

[4] Semple, p. 5.

and Mr. Marshall at one time baptized 42 persons. In August, 1760, a church was constituted under the pastoral care of the Rev. Dutton Lane. This was the first Separate Baptist church in Virginia, and in some sense the mother of all the rest." [5] This church seems to have been the Dan River church in Pittsylvania county. [6] "Soon after Mr. Lane's conversion," continues Semple, "the power of God was effectual in the conversion of Samuel Harriss, a man of great distinction in those parts." [7] "Samuel Harriss, commonly called Colonel Harriss, was born in Hanover county, Virginia, January 12th, 1724. Few men could boast of more respectable parentage. His education, though not the most liberal, was considerable for the customs of that day. When young, he moved to the county of Pittsylvania, and as he advanced in age, became a favorite with the people as well as with the rulers. He was appointed church warden, sheriff, a justice of the peace, burgess of the county, colonel of the militia, captain of Mayo fort, and commissary for the fort and army. All these things, however, he counted but dross, that he might win Christ Jesus and become a minister of His word among the Baptists, a sect at that time everywhere spoken against. . . . In 1759 he was ordained ruling elder. His labors were chiefly confined, for the first six or seven years, to the adjacent counties of Virginia and North Carolina, never having passed to the north of James River until the year 1765. [8] In January, 1765, upon the invitation of Allen Wyley, of Culpeper, a convert of the Regular Baptists, Harriss went to that county and preached the first day at Wyley's house. When he began to preach the next day, a mob appeared with whips, sticks and clubs, and so interfered that Harriss went that night over into Orange. Here he preached for many days to great crowds. In 1766 some of the young converts of these meetings went to Harriss's house to bring

---

[5] Ibid., p. 5.   [6] Beale's Semple, 17, 65.
[7] Semple, 5.   [8] Semple, Biography of Harriss.

him back to Orange. They soon returned, bringing with
them also the Rev. James Read of North Carolina. Arriv-
ing in Orange within the bounds of what became afterwards
the Blue Run Church, they found a large congregation
met together to whom they preached. The next day they
preached at Elijah Craig's to a 'vast crowd.' The 'Regular' preachers, Thomas and Garrard, were present also.
The Separates and the Regulars could not unite, and the
next day both parties held meetings and both baptized converts. Harriss and Read went on southerly through Spottsylvania into the upper parts of Caroline, Hanover, and
Goochland. The next year they returned, accompanied by
Dutton Lane. Together they constituted[9] the first Separate Baptist Church north of James River. This took
place on the 20th of November, 1767. The church was
called *Upper Spottsylvania*, and consisted of twenty-five
members, including all the Separate Baptists north of James
River. This was a mother to many other churches."[10]
Read and Harriss continued, we are told, their visits to
these parts of the country with remarkable results for about
three years longer, up to about 1770. They baptized sev-

---

[9] "*The Materials and Form of a Baptist Church.*—The Baptist
Church consists in a certain number of persons, called by the
Gospel out of the world, baptized on profession of their faith, and
federally united together, to worship GOD, and rule itself according
to His Word, independent of any other society whatever."
Thomas, The Virginian Baptist, p. 24.
  "*The Constitution of a Baptist Church.*—The constitution of a
Church is nothing else, but the solemn entrance of a number of
persons into Covenant as observed above and a public declaration
of their having done so. And to this end several things are
requisite, as: 1. A previous season of fasting and prayer. . . . 2.
Calling an orderly minister to their aid. . . . 3. An inquiry into
the qualifications of the candidate. . . . 4. A declaration of the
persons to be joined in covenant, showing their willing consent to
give themselves to the Lord, and to one another as a people
separated from the world . . . together with their hearty purpose
to reject all error, and avoid every wicked and unholy way."
Thomas, The Virginian Baptist, 26-27.
  [10] Semple, 10.

enty-five persons at one time, it is said, and as many as two
hundred on one of their journeys. Hundreds of men would
camp out all night on the ground in order to hear them the
next day. People travelled more than one hundred miles
to go to their meetings; to go forty or fifty miles was common. More churches were soon needed. " Accordingly,
on the second day of December, 1769, *Lower Spottsylvania
Church* was constituted with 154 members, who chose John
Waller for pastor. He was consecrated to this office June
2, 1770. Lewis Craig was consecrated pastor to the mother
church, November, 1770. *Blue Run Church* was constituted December 4, 1769, choosing Elijah Craig for their
pastor; he was consecrated May, 1771." [11]

The work now went rapidly forward. A popular tide
began to rise. Each new convert became a zealous mis-
sionary. The accepted preachers and leaders went hither
and thither incessantly. Jeremiah Moore said he had
" travelled and preached distances sufficient to reach twice
around the world." [12] Samuel Harriss " became almost a
constant traveller. Not confining himself to narrow limits,
but led on from place to place; wherever he could see an
opening to do good, there he would hoist the flag of peace.
There was scarcely any place in Virginia in which he did
not sow the Gospel seed." [13] To illustrate:

" Arrested in Culpeper and carried into court as a dis-
turber of the peace, he was ordered not to preach in the
county again within the twelvemonth on pain of going to
jail. From Culpeper he went into Fauquier and preached
at Carter's Run. From thence he crossed the Blue Ridge
and preached in Shenandoah. On his return from thence,
he turned in at Captain Thomas Clanahan's, in the county
of Culpeper, where there was a meeting. While certain
young ministers were preaching, the Word of God began
to burn in Colonel Harriss's heart. When they finished,

---

[11] Semple, 11.   [12] Ibid., 309.
[13] Semple, Biography of Harriss, 379.

he rose and addressed the congregation: ' I partly promised the devil, a few days past, at the courthouse, that I would not preach in this county again in the term of a year. But the devil is a perfidious wretch, and covenants with him are not to be kept; and, therefore, I will preach.' He preached a lively, animating sermon. The court never meddled with him more." [14]

These details concerning Samuel Harriss have been given for the two-fold purpose of showing the extreme activity of the Baptist missionaries in these years, and of illustrating the way in which the attacks upon these itinerant preachers began. In his own county, where he was known and respected, Harriss seems never to have been molested. The social element was in his favor. Thus, it is related of him that he wished to preach to the officers and soldiers. " An opportunity offered in Fort Mayo, and Mr. Harriss began his harangue, urging most vehemently the necessity of the new birth. In the course of his harangue, an officer interrupted him, saying: " Colonel, you have sucked up much eloquence from the rum cask to-day. Pray give us a little, that we may declaim as well when it comes to our turn." Harriss replied: " I am not drunk," and resumed his discourse. He had not gone far before he was accosted by another in a serious manner, who, looking in his face, said: " Sam, you say you are not drunk; pray, are you mad, then? What the devils ails you? " Colonel Harriss replied, in the words of Paul: " I am not mad, most noble gentleman." [15] Away from home, however, Harriss did not meet with the same courtesy from individuals. Indeed, it is evident that at first the masses of the people were opposed to the Baptists and feared them. The presence of the rabble is shown by the kind of attack made upon them. Some illustrations may make plainer the temper of the times. Speaking of the early work of the Regular Baptists in Northeastern Virginia, Semple says: " Sometimes when the

---

[14] Semple, ibid., 282.   [15] Semple, ibid., 381.

preachers came to a place for the purpose of preaching, a
kind of mob would be raised, and by violent threats they
hindered the preacher." [16]   Threats became blows.   Colonel
Harriss, Rev. John Koones and others were beaten with
clubs and cuffed and kicked and hauled about by the hair;
mobs ducked some preachers till they were nearly drowned;
a live snake and a hornet's nest were, upon different occa-
sions, thrown into the meetings to break them up; and
drunken ruffians insulted the preachers. [17]   That the
preachers were themselves partly responsible for this we
learn from what Semple says about them after the close of
the revival of 1785-92: "Their preachers were become
much more correct in their manner of preaching.   A great
many odd tones, disgusting whoops, and awkward gestures
were disused; in their matter also they had more of sound
sense and strong reasoning.   Their zeal was less mixed with
enthusiasm, and their piety became more rational." [18]   But
in the beginning they "whooped" in "many odd tones."
Leland tells us also that "The Separates were the most
zealous, and the work among them was very noisy.   The
people would cry out, fall down, and for a time lose the use
of their limbs, which exercise made the bystanders marvel;
some thought they were deceitful, others that they were
bewitched, and many, being convinced of all, would report
that God was with them of a truth." [19]   Some of these people, we are told, would be nervously affected; they had the
"jerks," [20] muscular contortions; they had the "barks,"
and yelped like dogs; they rolled on the ground in agonized
dread of hell-fire and eternal damnation, or they leaped
into the air with ecstatic shouts at the glory of their new-
found salvation.   We see here a frame of mind like that of
Bunyan when he heard voices warning him, or like that of
Balfour of Burley, with sharp sword out, lunging against

---

[16] Semple, 294.
[17] Semple, 20, 185, 382, 309, 357, 413: Fristoe, *passim.*
[18] Semple, 39.   [19] Leland, p. 105.   [20] Semple, 320, note.

the very devil himself.[21]   We seem, as we read, to be on the
verge of slipping back into the Middle Ages; of seeing
again the sailors of Columbus on their knees as they chant
the Gospel of John to ward off the oncoming water-spout;
of witnessing the dancing mania reproduced, or of hearing
again the enthusiastic shouts of the Crusading multitudes:
" Noel! Noel! God wills it! "   In truth, many of these people were but little removed from the Middle Ages in the
intensity of their religious emotion and belief.   The miraculous became to them the commonplace of God's chosen
ones, and the commonplace became miraculous.[22]

---

[21] Cf. Sir Walter Scott, " Old Mortality," ch. 43, and notes.

[22] " *Objection XIV.   Against making a Noise, etc., under Preaching.*
You pretend to stick very close to the word of GOD, to be sure!
But where, I pray ye, do you read of such noisy meetings!   What
loud crying!   What jumping up!   What falling down!   What
roaring, schreeching, screaming!   Does the Holy Scripture counte-
nance such wild disorder? . . . .
Answer.—As these horrid vociferations and obstreperous com-
motions, mentioned in the objection, never were the effect of my
preaching, nor are approved of by our churches, as any part of
religion; I am no ways obliged to vindicate any or all of them.
However, being it is cast upon the poor Baptists as an odium
peculiar to us, I shall give a short history of this modern phe-
nomenon, as follows:
The first appearance of it was under the preaching of the Rev.
George Whitefield, a noted priest of the Church of England, who
died two or three years ago, near Boston in New England.   From
him certain Presbyterians catched the fire, and zealously fanned
the flame for some years.   At last it kindled among some Baptists,
where it continues burning to this day.   Now, whether this fire is
celestial or terrestrial, or of what nature it is, as I pretend not to
know, I shall not undertake to determine.   Those who think it
is of GOD, are the fittest to defend it.   *They are of age, ask them,*
they shall speak for themselves.   I confess I can find no account of it
in the word of GOD."
Thomas, The Virginian Baptist, 63.
Evidently Thomas, and we may suppose the Regular Baptists
generally, disapproved of the " warm " and " enthusiastic " meetings of the Separates.
I remember being greatly impressed some years ago by the
remark of a young Swedish poet then visiting this country that
among the things which seemed most strange to him were the
absence of the folk songs and hymns and the presence of the (to

But those who were not swept along by this tide of emotion were both alarmed and angered by hope so exalted, by despair so abject, by zeal so intrusive. To many the very name Baptist was terrifying. They were thought to be sacrilegiously cruel in neglecting the baptism of their children, their own flesh and blood; and they were dreaded as monstrous beings. " . . . In the early part of my ministry," says Benedict, " a very honest and candid old lady, who had never been far from her retired home, said to me in a very sober tone: ' Your society are much more like other folk than they were when I was young. Then there was a company of them in the back part of our town, and an outlandish set of people they certainly were. For yourself would say so if you had seen them. As it was told to me, you could hardly find one among them but what was deformed in some way or other. Some of them were harelipped, others were blear-eyed, or hump-backed, or bowlegged, or clump-footed, hardly any of them looked like other people. But they were all strong for plunging, and let their poor ignorant children run wild, and never had the seal of the covenant put on them.' " [23]

With these things—strange to us—in mind, we can better understand why a woman should be whipped by her husband for being baptized by the Rev. John Leland, and why an ex-captain should draw his sword to kill Leland as he preached.[24] We can better understand, too, the feeling on

---

him) astonishing exhibitions of religious emotion witnessed in our camp-meetings and revivals. Of the last he wanted an explanation. I had none to offer. Matthew Arnold, in his essay " On the Study of Celtic Literature," maintains that this emotional religion of the English, as compared with the other Teutons, is due to the Celtic element. Perhaps some historico-philological Matthew Arnold in our midst may find in the sources of Virginia colonization and in the names of the early Virginia Baptists and Presbyterians some evidence of a Celtic influence present in those surprising revivals.

Cf. Matthew Arnold, On the Study of Celtic Literature, v, p. 94.

[23] Benedict, Fifty Years, 92 ff.

[24] Leland, Writings, 20, 27, etc.

the Baptist side that the avenging arm of the Lord was with them. Thus a child of Satan, a landlord, opened his house apparently to Leland's preaching but really to make money out of the crowds gathered to listen. Swiftly the wrath fell on him. "Some weeks afterwards . . . I saw the landlord's chimney standing but the house consumed by fire. When I saw it, my heart burst out in sacred language, Righteous art thou, Lord God Almighty, because thou hast judged thus!" [25] Upon another occasion, as "Robert Ware was preaching, there came one Davis and one Kemp, two sons of Belial, and stood before him with a bottle and drank, offering the bottle to him, cursing him. As soon as he closed his service, they drew out a pack of cards and began to play on the stage where he had been standing, wishing him to reprove them, that they might beat him." Now mark the sequel. "It is worthy of note that these two men both died soon after, ravingly distracted, each accusing the other of leading him into so detestable a crime." [26] The offence shows the popular feeling against the Baptist preachers; the punishment shows that the feeling has veered around in favor of the Baptists. So, too, when James Ireland was in jail in Culpeper county, "they attempted to blow him up with gunpowder, but the quantity obtained was only sufficient to force up some of the flooring of his prison. The individual who led in this infamous conduct was, shortly after, in a hunting excursion, and, while asleep in the woods, bitten by a mad wolf, of which wound he died in the most excruciating pain. There was also an attempt made by Elder Ireland's enemies to suffocate him by burning brimstone, etc., at the door and window of his prison. A scheme was also formed to poison him, but the mercy of God prevented." [27] We see the popular myth-making imagination in full swing here, and, as in the case cited above, on the Baptist side. The

---

[25] Leland, 23.   [26] Semple, 20, and note.
[27] J. B. Taylor, Virginian Baptist Ministers, 1st Series, 3d Edition, 1860, p. 120.

beasts of the field become the avengers of the Lord's anointed.

With the coming of the Separate Baptists north of James River, this opposition of the lower classes soon ceased. It was found that these men were reformers and not incendiaries. The people seem soon to have recognized that the Baptists were fighting their battles. After about 1770, the attacks and arrests were rarely made by the populace, and this year may be taken as roughly marking the popular reaction in favor of the Baptists and the beginning of the persecution by the civil authorities.

As we have already seen, Colonel Harriss was arrested and brought before the Court in Culpeper county; nor is it surprising that the civil authority should have laid hold of men whom their familiar acquaintances took to be either drunk or crazy, so new and strange seemed the manner and the matter of their talk. The magistrate who had Moore arrested while preaching (in Fairfax county, 1773) and ordered him to prison, wrote " his *mittimus* . . . in these remarkable words: ' I send you herewith the body of Jeremiah Moore, who is a preacher of the Gospel of Jesus Christ, and also a stroller.' " [28] When Waller and some others were arrested in Middlesex county, in 1771, the authorities " first searched their saddle-bags to find treasonable papers." [29] There were many honest, well-meaning people in Virginia to whom *Baptist* called up *Anabaptist* with a force that sent the cold shivers down their backs— and fear is proverbially cruel.[30]

" The first instance of actual imprisonment, we believe, that ever took place in Virginia, was in the county of Spottsylvania. On the fourth of June, 1768, John Waller, Lewis Craig, James Childs, etc., were seized by the sheriff

---

[28] Semple, 309.   [29] Ibid., 18.
[30] Fristoe, 65 ff., " They were charged with design . . . when once they supposed themselves sufficiently strong, that they would fall on their fellow subjects, massacre the inhabitants and take possession of the country."

and hauled before three magistrates, who stood in the meeting-house yard, and who bound them in the penalty of one
thousand pounds, to appear at the court two days after.
At court they were arraigned as disturbers of the peace.
. . . They (the Court) offered to release them if they would
promise to preach no more in the county for a year and a
day. This they refused, and, therefore, were sent into
close jail. As they were moving on from the courthouse
to the prison, through the streets of Fredericksburg they
sang the hymn—

'Broad is the road that leads to death,' etc.

This had an awful appearance." After four weeks confinement, Lewis Craig was released from prison, and immediately went down to Williamsburg to get a release for his
companions. He waited on the deputy-governor, the Hon.
John Blair, stated the case before him,[31] and received a

---

[31] This letter has been often referred to and sometimes quoted.
It deserves to be better known. The sidelight it throws upon
both the Established Church and the Baptists is interesting.

"*Sir:*—I lately received a letter, signed by a good number of
worthy gentlemen, who are not here, complaining of the Baptists;
the particulars of their misbehaviour are not told, any further than
their running into private houses and making dissensions. Mr.
Craig and Mr. Benjamin Waller are now with me, and deny the
charge; they tell me they are willing to take the oaths, as others
have. I told them I had consulted the Attorney-General who is of
opinion that the general court only have a right to grant licenses,
and, therefore, I referred them to the court. But on their application to the attorney-general, they brought me his letter, advising
me to write to you, that their petition was a matter of right, and
that you may not molest these conscientious people so long as
they behave themselves in a manner becoming pious Christians,
and in obedience to the laws, till the court, when they intend to
apply for license, and when the gentlemen, who complain, may
make their objections and be heard. The act of toleration (it being found by experience that persecuting dissenters increases their
numbers) has given them a right to apply, in a proper manner for
licensed houses, for the worship of God, according to their consciences; and I persuade myself, the gentlemen will quietly over-
look their meetings, till the Court. I am told they administer the
Sacrament of the Lord's supper near the manner we do, and

noble letter for the King's Attorney in Spottsylvania, in which the deputy-governor said that the prisoners had a right to petition the General Court for licenses and urged moderation and toleration of their meetings until the next meeting of the court. " When the letter came to the Attorney, he would have nothing to say in the affair. Waller and the others continued in jail forty-three days, and were then discharged without any conditions. While in prison they constantly preached through the grates. The mob without used every exertion to prevent the people from hearing, but to little purpose," [32] for converts were made notwithstanding.

This was a great triumph for the Baptist prisoners and their principles, a triumph at once over the civil authorities and over a hostile mob.

In like manner, in December, 1770, William Webber and Joseph Anthony went from Goochland across James River to Chesterfield and began preaching. They were promptly arrested and put into prison, where, as they refused to bind themselves, they staid until March following, in the meantime preaching through the prison grates to many people. [33]

Commenting on this occurrence, Campbell says: [34] " The persecutions of the Baptists commenced in Chesterfield in 1770, and in no county was it carried further. According to tradition, Colonel Archibald Cary, of Ampthill, was the

---

differ in nothing from our Church, but that of Baptism, and their renewing the ancient discipline, by which they have reformed some sinners and brought them to be truly penitent. Nay, if a man of theirs is idle and neglects to labor and provide for his family as he ought, he incurs their censures, which have had good effects. If this be their behaviour, it were to be wished we had some of it among us. But, at least, I hope all may remain quiet till the Court.

I am, with great respects to the Gentlemen, sir,

Your humble servant,

Williamsburg, July 16, 1768."   JOHN BLAIR.

Given by Semple, 15-16, and also found in Foote, Sketches of Virginia, i, 316, and elsewhere.

[32] Semple, 16-17.   [33] Semple, 17, ff.

[34] Campbell, History of Virginia, 555.

arch-persecutor. In few counties have the Baptists been more numerous than in Chesterfield."[35]

On August 10, 1771, William Webber and John Waller arrived in Middlesex on a course of meetings. That night about nine o'clock, with two others, James Greenwood and Robert Ware, they were lodged in the jail, which swarmed with fleas. They preached the next day, Sunday, in jail; and preached every Wednesday and Sunday to crowds. On the 24th they were taken into court and ordered to give bond for good behavior and not to preach in the county again for one year. On refusing, they were remanded to prison and fed on only bread and water for four days. They were liberated, on giving bond for good behavior, after forty-six days of confinement.

In August, 1772, James Greenwood and William Lovel were preaching in King and Queen county. They were seized, put in jail, kept there for sixteen days, until Court convened, and then discharged on giving bond for good behavior. On March 13, 1774, "the day on which Piscataway Church was constituted," John Waller, John Shackleford and Robert Ware were imprisoned in Essex county, remaining in jail until Court day, March 21, when Ware and Shackleford gave bond for good behavior for twelve months. Waller refused, was imprisoned fourteen days longer, then gave bond, and went home.[36]

---

[35] Semple, writing in 1809 the history of the Middle District Association, says on this subject: "This makes five Baptist churches already mentioned in the county of Chesterfield. And most of them large and respectable. It is worthy of remark, that generally the Baptist cause has flourished most extensively where it met with most severe opposition in the offset. In Chesterfield jail seven preachers were confined for preaching, viz., William Webber, Joseph Anthony, Augustine Eastin, John Weatherford, John Tanner, Jeremiah Walker and David Tinsley. Some were whipped by individuals, several fined. They kept up their persecution after other counties had laid it aside. They have now in the county more than 500 in communion, among whom are four magistrates, two majors, and five captains." Semple, 207.

[36] Semple, 17.

About a month later, on the second Saturday in May, 1774, the Association met at Hall's in Halifax county. "Letters were received at the Association from preachers confined in prison, particularly from David Tinsley, then confined in Chesterfield jail. The hearts of the brethren were affected at their sufferings, in consequence of which it was agreed to raise contributions for them. The following resolution was also entered into: 'Agreed to set apart the second and third Saturday in June as public fast days in behalf of our poor blind persecutors, and for the releasement of our brethren.'"[37] The effect on the public mind of such fast days so ordered must have been great.

Other similar cases of imprisonment might be cited. Between 1768 and 1775 inclusive, there seem to have been about thirty-four imprisonments. "About thirty of the preachers," according to Leland, "were honored with a dungeon, and a few others besides. Some of them were imprisoned as often as four times, besides all the mobs and perils they went through. The dragon roared with hideous peals but was not *red*—the Beast appeared formidable, but was not *scarlet-colored*. Virginia soil has never been stained with vital blood for conscience sake."[38]

---

[37] Semple, 56. These radical Baptists did a very curious thing in their Association held in the autumn of this year, 1774. They appointed Samuel Harriss, for the Southern District, and John Waller and Elijah Craig, for the Northern District, "Apostles" to superintend the churches and report to the next Association. Semple gravely observes: "These Apostles made their report to the next Association rather in discouraging terms, and no others ever were appointed. The judicious reader will quickly discover that this is only the old plan of bishops, etc., under a new name. In the last decision it was agreed that the office of apostles, like that of prophets, was the effect of miraculous inspiration, and did not belong to ordinary times" (p. 59). Thus exit the Baptist "Apostles," but the Baptist Church made a narrow escape. The episode illustrates the immense power of the forms of institutions to persist and to compel imitation.

[38] Leland, Writings, 107. Rev. C. F. James, in his "Documentary History of the Struggle for Religious Liberty in Virginia" (see *Religious Herald,* Jan. 5, 1899, Richmond, Va.), has collected these

Dr. Hawks, the historian of the Episcopal Church, comments thus: " The ministers (says Leland) were imprisoned, and the disciples buffeted. This is but too true. No dissenters in Virginia experienced for a time harsher treatment than did the Baptists. They were beaten and imprisoned; and cruelty taxed its ingenuity to devise new modes of punishment and annoyance. The usual consequences followed; persecution made friends for its victims; and the men who were not permitted to speak in public, found willing auditors in the sympathizing crowds who gathered around the prisons to hear them preach from the grated windows." [39]

It is to be observed that these arrests were made on peace warrants. The Baptists contended that this was a subterfuge; that the real persecutor was the Established Church; that there was no law for their arrest; and that they had all the rights of Dissenters in England under the toleration act. A very significant comment upon this claim was made

---

names in a paragraph, as follows: " In December, 1770, William Webber and Joseph Anthony were imprisoned in Chesterfield jail, and in May, 1774, David Tinsley, Augustine Eastin, John Weatherford, John Tanner, and Jeremiah Walker were imprisoned in the same jail. In Middlesex county, William Webber, John Waller, James Greenwood, and Robert Ware were imprisoned in August, 1771. (Semple, pp. 17, 18.) In Caroline county, Lewis Craig, John Burrus, John Young, Edward Herndon, James Goodrich, and Bartholomew Chewning were imprisoned, but the year is not given. (See Taylor's Virginia Baptist Ministers, vol. i, pp. 81, 82.) In King and Queen county, James Greenwood and William Lovel were imprisoned in August, 1772, and John Waller, John Shackleford, Robert Ware, and Ivison Lewis in March, 1774. (See Semple, p. 22.) Dr. Taylor, in his sketch of Elijah Craig, says he was imprisoned in Orange county, but does not give the year. According to Taylor's Virginia Baptist Ministers, there were confined in Culpeper jail, at different times, James Ireland, John Corbeley, Elijah Craig, Thomas Ammon, Adam Banks and Thomas Maxfield."

Dr. G. S. Bailey says " The father of Henry Clay was thus imprisoned, as a Baptist minister, in Virginia, as I was informed by Rev. Porter Clay, a brother of Henry Clay." Cf. " Trials and Victories of Religious Liberty in America," p. 40.

[39] Hawks, Protestant Episcopal Church in Virginia, p. 121.

by the House of Delegates in its action in 1778. On November 14 of that year, a petition of Jeremiah Walker, one
of the most prominent of the Baptist preachers and at that
time in good standing with his people, was presented praying for the reconsideration of " his being taxed with prison
charges " for the time he was in jail in Chesterfield county
in 1773 and 1774 " for preaching." The petition was referred to the Committee for Religion. On November 20,
the Committee brought in a resolution, That the petition
of Jeremiah Walker for refunding the value of prison fees
levied on him for the time " whilst confined in the jail ot
Chesterfield county for a breach of the peace," be rejected.
The resolution was read, amended, agreed to, and the petition rejected, the House endorsing the view that Walker's
offence had been a breach of the peace.[40] This action was
taken in the midst of the Revolution when all the help of
all the Baptists was needed.

It is to be observed, also, that these persecutions took
place chiefly in the older counties, that is, in the counties
lying along the great rivers of tidewater Virginia and in the
northeastern part of the colony. This is just the country
and the society that bred the men who led the Revolution,
and we remember that among the staunchest patriots were
some who at first were strong for the mother country and
for the Mother Church. This is the section of country also
in which were found the most worthless as well as some of
the best of the ministers of the Established Church. There
was, accordingly, a sharp clash of ecclesiastical interests
as well as of theological opinions in these parishes. A
review of the course of these events, however, renders it
exceedingly doubtful if, as a class, the ministers themselves
of the Established Church took an active part in the persecutions, though the Baptists believed so.[41] But the

---

[40] Journal of House of Delegates, November 14 and 20, 1778.

[41] Semple, 119, cites the friendly offer of a clergyman of one of
the parishes in Caroline to be security for Waller and Craig while
in Fredericksburg jail, if they wished to give bond.

Church Establishment, as an institution bound up with the political organization of Virginia society, was largely responsible for them.

Along the mountain border there were but few instances of persecution after the first year or two, and almost none in what were then the southwestern counties, nor any south of James River as a whole, Chesterfield county excepted.

Under such conditions of mind of the Virginia public and of the Baptists themselves, let us see what was the progress made by them, and the causes as well as the results of their growth.

The year 1770 may be taken as the starting point for this examination. In that year, the Separate Baptists of Virginia, North Carolina and South Carolina, after about ten or twelve years [42] of joint association meeting, decided to divide and to hold thenceforward their associations in their respective colonies.[43] ". . . At the commencement of the year 1770," says Semple, "there were but two [three] [44] Separate churches in all Virginia north of James river; and we may add, there were not more than about four on the south side." [45] In addition to these, in 1770, as we have already seen, there was one church in southeastern Virginia, and the Regular Baptists had ten churches, chiefly in the northeastern part of the colony.

This year, 1770, furnishes also the first petition from the Baptists to the Colonial Legislature for religious relief. The Journal of the House of Burgesses for May 26, 1770, contains " A petition of several persons, being Protestant dissenters of the Baptist persuasion, whose names are thereunto subscribed, was presented to the House and read, setting forth the inconveniences of compelling their licensed preachers to bear arms under the militia law and to attend musters, by which they are unable to perform the duties

---

[42] Backus, History of Baptists of N. E., iii, 274; Bitting, Strawberry Assn., 9, note.

[43] Semple, 47.   [44] Compare Semple, pp. 11 and 25.   [45] Semple, 25.

of their function, and further setting forth the hardships
they suffer from the prohibition to their ministers to preach
in meeting-houses, not particularly mentioned in their
licenses; and, therefore, praying the House to take their
grievances into consideration, and to grant them relief."

This petition evidently came from the Regular Baptists,
whose ministers were regularly licensed, as was not the
case ordinarily, if ever, with the Separate Baptists at this
time.

The petition was referred to the " Committee for Religion," which reported in a few days, June 1, " *Resolved,*
That it is the opinion of this committee that so much of
the said petition as prays that the ministers or preachers of
the Baptist persuasion may not be compelled to bear arms
or attend musters, be rejected."

The resolution was adopted by the House.[46]

The first session of the Virginia Separate Baptist Association was held at Craig's Meeting-house in Orange county
in May, 1771. Delegates from fourteen churches were
present, representing thirteen hundred and eighty-five members.[47] It is not known what was done at the meeting in
1772. At the session held in 1773, a division of the association was made into two districts, one north and one south
of James River.[48] Now the years from 1768 to 1774 inclusive were the time of the greatest persecution of the Baptists in Virginia. How little it availed is shown by the
records of these District Association meetings. In 1774
the Northern District met at Carter's Run in Fauquier
county in May, and letters were received from *twenty-four*
churches reporting a membership of 1921; the Southern
District held its second session at Walker's Meeting-house
in Amelia county in October, and letters were received from
thirty churches reporting a membership of 2083, a total of
over four thousand members. This total does not include

[46] Journal, House of Burgesses, May 26, June 1, 1770.
[47] Semple, 49; Bitting, Strawberry Assn., 12, says twelve churches.
[48] Ibid., 55 ff.

the membership of any Separate churches not sending delegates to these two meetings; nor does it include the four
churches in southeastern Virginia—three new since 1770,
two in Sussex and one in Isle of Wight,[49] with a membership of over 150; nor does it include the fourteen churches
of the Regular Baptists—four new since 1770, two in Fauquier, one in Frederick, one in the Redstone Settlement
(Great Bethel, Monongalia county, Virginia)[50] with a membership of about 800. Making these additions, we get ap-
proximately five thousand as the number of Baptist church
members in Virginia in the fall of 1774. Such a growth is
astonishing: from eighteen or nineteen churches, with something like eight hundred and fifty members in 1770, to
seventy-two churches, with a membership of over five thousand in the fall of 1774, less than five years.[51]

The causes of such popular religious movements it is not
easy to ascertain and to state precisely. As we read this story,
we are reminded of the Puritan movement in England; of
the Wicklifites in the fourteenth century; even of the Bare-
foot Friars of the thirteenth century. The resemblance is
a general one. More particularly, in the case of the Virginia Baptists, we doubtless see an outgrowth of that same
principle of Protestant evolution which, beginning formally
with the Reformation, culminated in the latter half of the
eighteenth and the early part of the nineteenth centuries
in the immense development of the Methodists. This is the
principle of direct personal communion with God, of independent soul-experience. Its last great impulse in England
and America came with the preaching of the Wesleys and
Whitefield. As "The Great Awakening,"[52] it made for

---

[49] Semple, 343.   [50] Fristoe, 9.

[51] I am unable to say whether any, and if so how many, of these
members were negroes; possibly a few. The impression left by the
works of Leland, Semple, Benedict, and others is, I think, that
the negroes did not begin to come into the churches until somewhat later, unless in very small numbers.

[52] Tracy, The Great Awakening.

itself a distinctive name in America, and called forth the
zeal of " New Lights " and " Old Lights " in both conti-
nents. The development of this principle is the third
broadly distinctive phase of the evolution of Christianity,
the first phase being dogmatic, the second that of the great
institutional church.[53]

---

[53] Bryce, Holy Roman Empire, 325 ff.
" . . . but (the Reformation) was also something more profound
and fraught with mightier consequences than any of them. It was
in its essence the assertion of the principle of individuality—that is
to say, of true spiritual freedom. Hitherto the personal consciousness had been a faint and broken reflection of the universal,
obedience had been held the first of religious duties; truth had
been conceived as a something external and positive, which the
priesthood who were its stewards were to communicate to the
passive layman, and whose saving virtue lay not in its being felt
and known by him to be truth, but in a purely formal and unreason-
ing acceptance. . . . The universal consciousness became the Visible
Church: the Visible Church hardened into a government and
degenerated into a hierarchy. . . . All this system of doctrine . . .
was suddenly rent in pieces by the convulsion of the Reformation,
and flung away by the more religious and more progressive peo-
ples of Europe. That which was external and concrete was in
all things to be superseded by that which was inward and spiritual.
It was proclaimed that the individual spirit, while it continued to
mirror itself in the world-spirit, had nevertheless an independent
existence as a centre of self-issuing force, and was to be in all
things active rather than passive. Truth was no longer to be
truth to the soul until it should have been by the soul recognized
and in some measure even created; but when so recognized and
felt, it is able under the form of faith to transcend outward works
and to transform the dogmas of the understanding; it becomes
the living principle within each man's breast, infinite itself, and
expressing itself infinitely through his thoughts and acts. He who
as a spiritual being was delivered from the priest, and brought
into direct relation with the Divinity, needed not, as heretofore,
to be enrolled a member of a visible congregation of his fellows,
that he might live a pure and useful life among them. Thus by
the Reformation the Visible Church as well as the priesthood lost
that paramount importance which had hitherto belonged to it,
and sank from being the depositary of all religious tradition, the
source and centre of religious life, the arbiter of eternal happiness or misery, into a mere association of Christian men, for the
expression of mutual sympathy and the better attainment of certain
common ends."

To that part of the Virginia people who then became
Baptists, this vitalizing principle of religious life did not
seem to be in the Established Church, which neglected
them; nor among the Quakers, who had long since covered
it over with the veil of that rigid informal formality which
still parts them from their fellow-citizens; nor in Presbyte-
rianism, with its intellectual demands of an elaborate creed.
These people needed a distinctive symbol and a compara-
tively formless faith; they found the one in adult baptism
by immersion, and the other in the wide compass of Bible
teaching, wherein the devout and emotional soul finds what
it seeks.   Among them, accordingly, as Leland tells us,
some " held to predestination, others to universal provision; some adhered to a confession of faith, others would
have none but the Bible; some practised laying on of hands,
others did not." [54]   They agreed among themselves to dis-
agree; and they held together in their churches.

Another cause of the rapid spread of Baptist doctrine and
association was social.[55]   The Established Church was the
rich man's church unworthily administered; the Quakers
were exclusive.   The plain, ignorant people would none
of either of these, for their wants were not satisfied by
them.   They wanted an organization, a ministry, a preaching, responsive to their own manner of thought and to their

---

The Rev. Dr. S. D. McConnell, of Holy Trinity Church, Brook-
lyn, read some years ago before the Contemporary Society of
Philadelphia a valuable paper on "The Next Phase of Christianity," in which he maintained that the next or fourth phase of
Christianity was the practical one of the religion of conduct, as
distinguished from dogmatism, institutionalism, and personal religion.

[54] Leland quoted by Hawks, Protestant Episcopal Church in
Virginia, 122.

[55] Tidewater Virginia, we must remember, was emphatically
Cavalier Virginia.

"The great Cavalier exodus began with the King's execution
in 1649, and probably slackened after 1660.   It must have been a
chief cause of the remarkable increase of the white population of
Virginia from 15,000 in 1649 to 38,000 in 1670."   Fiske, ii, 16.

emotions. The Baptist organization supplied the demands of their thought and their emotion, and on a plane congenial to their habit of speech and of life. Now, social classes were sharply defined in Virginia in 1770, and the assertion by unlettered men of the right to think for themselves and to lead others was first ridiculed and then resented. After due allowance has been made for civil alarm and ecclesiastical jealousy, it seems certain that there was, during those early years and down into the practical beginnings of the Revolution, say in 1774-1775, a strong current of social antagonism setting against the Baptists, and, of course, a corresponding feeling on the part of the Baptists for those hostile to them. Fristoe says, speaking of the years prior to 1774: " The cant word was they are an ignorant, illiterate set—and of the poor and contemptible class of the people." [56] Born about 1748 in Stafford county, converted very early in life, preaching at nineteen, chosen moderator of his Association at twenty-six, Fristoe had lived through the struggle and seen its successful issue when, at sixty years of age, he published his book in 1808. The Rev. John Waller, so noted afterwards as a Baptist preacher, illustrates both phases of the situation; for as wild, " Swearing Jack Waller," the dissolute member of a well-known family, he was one of the Grand Jury that presented Lewis Craig for disturbing the peace by his preaching. Leland, probably the ablest man in the Baptist ministry in Virginia during the Revolution, comments with ill-concealed contempt in his " Virginia Chronicle " (p. 117), on the cropped heads of the Baptist men and the plain dress of the women; and Semple, speaking of Leland's call to the pastorate of Mount Poney Church in 1777, says: " The habits of the Baptists in New England and of those in Virginia respecting apparel were also much at variance. Mr. Leland and others adhered to the customs of New England, each one putting on such apparel as suited his own fancy. This was

---

[56] Fristoe, History of Ketocton Association, 64.

offensive to some members of the Church. The contention on this account became so sharp that on the twenty-fifth of July, 1779, about twelve members dissented from the majority of the Church, and were of course excluded." [57]

The first attempts (1768-1769) to bring together the Regulars and the Separates were defeated by this matter of dress apparently. "Among the Separates, the objections raised by a few popular characters prevailed. They, it seems, thought the Regulars were not sufficiently particular in small matters, such as dress, etc." [58] So, too, in 1773, Elijah Craig and David Thomson, delegates from the General Association of Virginia to the Kehukee Association (August, 1773) in Halifax county, North Carolina, stated among objections "to a communion with them. . . . Secondly, they were, as they alleged, too superfluous in their dress; contending that excessive dress ought to be made a matter of church discipline." [59] This reads like a chapter from Puritan England. Contrast it with what Semple says of the Baptists twenty years later, in 1792: "They were much more numerous and, of course, in the eyes of the world, more respectable. Besides, they were joined by persons of much greater weight in civil society. . . . This could not but influence their manners and spirit more or less. Accordingly, a great deal of that simplicity and plainness, that rigid scrupulosity about little matters, which so happily tends to keep us at a distance from greater follies, was laid aside." [60]

Evidently we are dealing with a social upheaval as well as with a religious and political revolution. As this became plainer to the contemporary generation, more and more members of the well-to-do and intelligent classes began to join the Baptists, so that with the opening of the Revolution the attitude of the denomination before the public was already changed. The "cant word" that so vexed Fristoe was no longer true in the manner and to the ex-

---

[57] Semple, 177-178.   [58] Semple, 45-46.   [59] Ibid., 349.   [60] Semple, 39.

tent that it had been. This change continued increasingly during the course of the war and left the Baptists at its close, as Semple says, " in the eyes of the world more respectable."

The economic cause was also at work; had been at work for years. That had been the mainspring in bringing about the victory in the famous " Parsons' Cause " in 1763, when all the laity of Virginia stood together as against the Establishment. The irritation from that old burden was intensified by the new theological antagonism. " To pay taxes," they said within themselves, " to a set of lazy parsons was hard to bear when a man was still in the bonds of iniquity; but for a man who had learned to dwell within the gates of Zion to pay taxes to this bastard brood of the Scarlet Woman, was abominable. The servants of the Lord who daily went in and out before them, ministering to their spiritual wants, received no worldly reward save as free-will offering;[61] and yet they must feed fat these ravening wolves in sheep's clothing. It was intolerable."

It is perhaps not too much to say that the Virginia Baptists of 1774 deserve credit for not breaking out into the excesses of mob violence.

---

[61] The Separate Baptists at first disapproved sternly of their ministers receiving any salary. This was the natural result of their religious enthusiasm and of their hostility to the salaried clergy. Its inconveniences were soon felt. Taylor repeats a pathetic story (taken from " The Baptist," Tenn., R. B. C. Howell, Editor), which " if not true is well found," of the pitiful condition to which a young farmer-preacher's zeal had reduced his family. They were found in a state of destitution by the famous Samuel Harriss, the very man who had denounced hireling ministers and who was responsible for this young preacher's conduct, but who now saw the error of his former opinion. J. B. Taylor, Virginia Baptist Ministers, 1st Series, 37.

" The Maintenance of the Ministry.

As gospel ministers should not, if it can be helped, entangle themselves with the affairs of their life, but spend all their time in watching over and providing food for the flocks committed to their care, so it is most reasonable, that they should be supported as to temporal things, by those who enjoy their labors." Thomas, The Virginian Baptist, 25.

This Regular view is in sharp contrast to the early Separate view.

In fact, this economic cause had a hundred years before been largely instrumental in bringing about Bacon's Rebellion, of which the Baptist uprising against the Establishment during the Revolutionary period may be regarded as the final outcome. The law of March, 1662,[62] which changed the Vestry from an elective body to a self-perpetuating close corporation in the hands of the landowners, was abrogated by Bacon's Assembly in 1676, was revived by the next Assembly in 1677, and was the object of prolonged and successful attack by the Dissenters during the Revolution. This is not surprising when we remember that the Vestry " apportioned the taxes, elected the church-wardens, who were in many places the tax-collectors, ' processioned ' the bounds of lands, thus affecting the record of land-titles, supervised the counting of tobacco, and presented the minister for induction." [63]

The Vestry therefore touched the sensitive pocket nerve on all sides, and was correspondingly detested by those who had no share in its selection or its deliberations, and who had come to differ from its members in religious opinion. As we shall see, the economic struggle against what had been the Established Church continued long after religious freedom had been attained.

A fourth cause, more powerful than any one of those mentioned, as taking them all, in part, up into itself, was political. Liberty was getting to be in the air—liberty, the heritage of his race, all the dearer to the poor man in that he was poor. And yet he had to submit to be married, to have his father buried, to have his child baptized by the minister, often scandalously unfit, of a lordly church which forced from him his hated tithes, and whose clergy were even now (April-June, 1771) trying to make it more aristocratic by the institution of an American Bishopric. Now the

---

[62] Hening, ii, 44-45.

[63] For an interesting discussion of this subject in connection with Bacon's Rebellion, cf. Fiske, Old Virginia, ii, 96 ff.

Baptist organization is the most democratic [64] of the great
Protestant bodies. Each church is a little republic in which
each member has his rights and may maintain them among
his fellows. Such a system appealed powerfully to the political instincts of the Virginian of those days, as was
proved by the sympathy for and with the Baptists shown by
Henry, Jefferson, Madison, and other representative men.[65]

Thus urged by their religious, social, economic, and political likes and dislikes, the plain people of Virginia flocked
into the Baptist Church and were only exasperated, not
hindered, by the persecution to which their leaders were
subjected.

The greatest gains made during this short period were

---

[64] " *The government of the Baptist Church.*—. . . Being a distinct
body, or corporation, it is entrusted with the whole prerogative of
judicature respecting itself. . . . (1) We have particular meetings
appointed . . . every member is to attend. . . . (2) We allow none
to be present but our own members. . . . (3) At these meetings we
meddle not with any state affairs. No; we leave such things to
the Commonwealth to which alone they belong. We concern not
ourselves with the government of the colony; nor any point relating to it; unless it be to pray for both the temporal and eternal
welfare of all the inhabitants. We form no intrigues. We lay no
schemes to advance ourselves, nor make any attempts to alter the
constitution of the Kingdom to which we belong. . . . (4) At these
meetings we consider and adjust all matters relating to the peace,
order and edification of the Church. . . . We enquire into the conduct of our members, . . . acquit the innocent, receive the penitent,
and pass judgment upon all irreclaimable offenders . . . and the
incorrigible . . . are excommunicated." Thomas, The Virginian
Baptist, 31-33.
This was doubtless a perfectly sincere statement when Thomas
wrote it in 1773. But compare it with what Semple says about
petitions to overturn the Church Establishment towards the close
of 1774,[a] and with the proposal of the Committee of the Regular
Baptists in 1780 to the General Association as to national grievances,[b] and with the whole history of the General Committee.[c]
Times change, and we change with them.
[65] Curry, J. L. M., Establishment and Disestablishment, 94. "The
fact is incontestable, that religious and political ameliorations are
contemporaneous, and have been accomplished by the same persons."

---

[a] See p. 27 ff.   [b] See p. 52.   [c] See pp. 54-69.

in those parts of Virginia, the oldest and most thickly settled, in which the Established Church had been longest
given its opportunity of doing good: In tidewater and
lower Virginia—in James City county (first home of Eng-
lishmen in Virginia), in King and Queen, Middlesex, Essex,
Caroline, Goochland, Louisa, Spottsylvania,* Stafford;*
over the Blue Ridge—in Frederick,* Berkeley,* Shenandoah,* Rockingham;* back in Piedmont Virginia, along the
eastern slopes of the Blue Ridge—in Loudoun,* Fauquier,*
Culpeper, Madison, Orange,* Albemarle, Fluvanna, Amherst; across the James River in Southside Virginia—in
Buckingham, Prince Edward, Charlotte, Bedford, Franklin;
on the North Carolina border—in Henry, Pittsylvania,*
Halifax,* Mecklenburg; thence northerly and easterly—in
Lunenburg, Nottoway,* Amelia, Powhatan, Chesterfield,
Dinwiddie, Sussex, Isle of Wight, and so to Princess Anne*
and the Atlantic Ocean. In thirteen (those marked with
the asterisk) of these thirty-nine counties, possibly in more,
the Baptists had effected some sort of lodgment before
1770, in these they increased their numbers. In the remaining twenty-six counties they established churches
for the first time after 1770 (as far as I can ascertain),
though itinerant preachers went through many, perhaps
all, of these counties also at an earlier date, making many
converts as they went.[66]

However that may be, the Baptists constituted in 1774 a
large body of the people inspired by a new-born zeal, ani-
mated by an almost fierce spirit of proselytism, organized
into vigorous and widely distributed branches with cen-
tralized organ of common action, and held together by a
common resistance and hatred of their spiritual oppressor
the Established Church.

These people were formidable in numbers, though it is
hard to determine just how numerous they were. Benedict,

---

[66] The names of the counties are given as they stand in Semple
(in 1809-10). Many of these counties were not laid off in 1774 (see
map).

writing in 1813, after prolonged travels among his co-relig-
ionists, says: " From the many observations I have made
on the spread of Baptist principles, I am inclined to think,
that without counting that class in Massachusetts and Con-
necticut, who hang to the denomination merely by certifi-
cates, we may reckon seven adherents to one communi-
cant." [67] According to this estimate, the five thousand Virginia Baptist members in 1774 would find themselves supported by an army of thirty-five thousand sympathizers in
a total population of probably 400,000 free inhabitants—
about one in every ten. That estimate seems high. But
taking two-thirds or even one-half of this number as a correct estimate,[68] we can easily understand the politico-relig-

---

[67] David Benedict, A General History of the Baptist Denomination, Boston, 1813, vol. ii, p. 553.

[68] Note on Population of Virginia and Number of Baptists. It
is not possible to do more than approximate the number of people
in Virginia at this time. The " Virginia Almanac " for 1776 gives
(p. 2) " An estimate of the number of souls in the following prov-
inces, made in Congress, September, 1774:

In Massachusetts	400,000
New Hampshire	150,000
Rhode Island	59,678
Connecticut	192,000
New York	250,000
New Jersey	130,000
Pennsylvania	350,000
Maryland	320,000
Virginia	650,000
North Carolina	300,000
South Carolina	225,000
Total	3,026,678

Leland says in his *Virginia Baptist Chronicle*, which was published in Virginia in 1790, " Mr. Jefferson says, that in 1782, there
were in this State 567,614 inhabitants, of every age, sex and condition. Of which 296,852 were free, and 270,762 were slaves. . . .
Mr. Randolph, in 1788, stated the round numbers . . . (at) 588,000.
These gentlemen had both official accounts being both governors
of Virginia, but the returns from the counties are imperfect, and
from some counties no returns at all are made to the executive."
The census report of 1790 gives the number for Virginia as: free
whites, 442,117; other free persons, 12,863; slaves, 292,627; total,

ious agitation that now began. " So favorable did their prospects appear," says Semple, " that towards the close of the year 1774, they began to entertain serious hopes, not

---

747,610. The population would be likely to decrease during the Revolutionary War because of the war, and still more, both during and after the war, because of the rapid emigration to Kentucky.

The number of Baptists likewise can only be approximated. Leland says: " There were a few Baptists in Virginia before the year 1760, but they did not spread so as to be taken notice of by the people, much less by the rulers, till after that date."

The churches increased in number from eighteen in 1770 to about ninety in 1776, and it seems altogether probable that the number of members was not far from as large then as it was for some years afterwards, owing to the constant emigration to Kentucky.

In 1790, Leland says there were " 1 General Committee; 11 associations; 202 churches; 150 ministers; 20,000 members."[a]

Rippon's *Baptist Register*, under the heading " A View of the Baptist Associations, etc., in the United States of America and Vermont for October, 1790 " (p. 72), gives the following table of Associations and the comment thereon:

	Ministers	Churches	Members
Ketocton*	10	12	650
Chappawamsic*	7	14	850
Orange District*	22	32	4600
Dover District*	36	26	5100
Lower District and Kehukee*..	45	51	5500
Middle District*	24	25	2000
Roanoke and North Carolina*..	18	18	2200
S. Kentucky*	15	14	1200
N. Kentucky	10	12	1100
Ohio	4	5	300

The nine associations in the above list marked with asterisks meet in a General Committee by their representatives at Richmond in the month of May annually. Due allowance being made for North Carolina, North Kentucky and Ohio in this list, the results conform fairly to the estimate of Leland.

Semple says: " Asplund's Register for 1791, soon after the great revival, makes the number of Baptists 20,439 in Virginia." [b]

Benedict, after prolonged travel and consideration of the subject, thinks (1860) that " in 1800 there were only about 80,000 Baptists in North America and about 20,000 in Virginia." [c]

A more recent authority still, Armitage (1887), concludes that " as nearly as we can get at the figures, there were but 97 Baptist

---

[a] Leland, Writings, 117.   [b] Semple, 446.
[c] Benedict, Fifty Years among Baptists.

only of obtaining liberty of conscience, but of actually over-
turning the Church establishment, from whence all their
oppressions had arisen. Petitions for this purpose were

---

churches in all the colonies in 1770. . . . in 1784 our total membership in the thirteen colonies was only about 35,000 "; [a] and that:
" We find that while the first Church was planted in that Colony
(Virginia) in 1714, in 1793 there were in the State 227 churches,
272 ministers, 22,793 communicants, and 14 associations." [b]

Semple closes his estimate of the number—thirty-one thousand
and fifty-two—of Baptists in Virginia at the time of his writing
(1809), by saying: " The increase in nineteen years (since 1790) is
more than fifty per cent. During this period it has been supposed
that over one-fourth of the Baptists of Virginia have moved to
Kentucky and other parts of the western country." [c] And Semple
remarks elsewhere: " It is questionable with some whether half of
the Baptist preachers who have been raised in Virginia have not
emigrated to the western country." [d] This emigration westward
is the subject of constant remark by the Baptist writers of the
times. Lewis Craig went to Kentucky in 1781. " In removing
from Virginia," says Taylor, " he had taken with him most of the
members of the Upper Spottsylvania, since called Craig's church.
This was the oldest and most flourishing body of baptized be-
lievers between James and Rappahannock rivers. . . . The pastor
and flock, numbering about two hundred members, and called by
John Taylor ' the travelling church,' commenced their long toil-
some journey. The whole, embracing children and servants, num-
bered nearly four hundred." [e] Rev. Lewis Lunsford, in a letter
under date of March 11, 1793, written after his return from Kentucky, says: " The emigration to that country is incredible." [f]

In view of the number of churches in 1776, in view also of the
estimates cited and of the continuous emigration to Kentucky, it
seems probable that there were at the end of 1775 something like
10,000 Baptist members in Virginia, and that the number rapidly
rose to about 20,000 and remained near those figures till the end
of the century. This is a mere guess, however. The estimate as
to churches is likewise a guess. It is based on Semple's tables,
which in turn are based on Asplund's Register, in part, on Fristoe's
History, and on the Association records. But Semple gives names
not found in Fristoe for the corresponding period, and he omits

---

[a] Thos. Armitage, History of the Baptists, N. Y., 1887, p. 776.

[b] Thos. Armitage, History of Baptists, 735.

[c] Semple, 446.

[d] Semple, 172.

[e] J. B. Taylor, Virginia Baptist Ministers, First Series, 3d ed.,
N. Y., 1860, 89.

[f] Taylor, ibid., 142.

accordingly drawn and circulated with great industry. Vast numbers, readily, and indeed, eagerly, subscribed to them." [69] Thenceforward, the Baptists pursued the Church Establishment with a vindictive hatred that is repellent, however natural it may have been, and however glad we may be that the Establishment was finally destroyed.

The cause of this hatred has already been stated in part. We have seen that a strong social element was one of the formative influences of the Baptist organization at this particular time. That it is easy for the upper class of society to misunderstand and despise those below, and for the lower class to hate those above, has been abundantly shown in history before and since the French Revolution. [70] At this early time very few of the Baptists belonged to the aristocratic, office-holding class which filled the county courts, which furnished the members of the parish vestries, and which, therefore, levied taxes upon these, their poor neighbors, for the support of an official church grossly neglectful of its sacred duties. This class feeling was increased by the Established clergy, themselves members of the upper class in virtue of their position and in so many cases unworthy of either class or position.

What Semple says on this subject is but the common testimony of the times: " The great success and rapid increase of the Baptists in Virginia, must be ascribed primarily to the power of God working with them. Yet it cannot be

---

names found in Fristoe. The absence of the date of foundation of so many churches in his tables renders the matter still more confused and confusing; and finally he himself complains despairingly, " Churches used so often to change their names that it is now really difficult to identify an old church." To this may be added, that churches seemed to be abandoned and to be revived in a manner beyond the calculus of probabilities. An approximation seems to be as near as we can come to the fact; but the fact was very substantial.   [69] Semple, 25.

[70] Let whoever would better understand this social class attitude of the middle of the XVIII Century read—and read between the lines—Fielding's " Tom Jones," as well as " The Spectator," and Goldsmith.

denied but that there were subordinate and cooperating causes; one of which, and the main one, was the loose and immoral deportment of the established clergy, by which the people were left almost destitute of even the shadow of true religion. 'Tis true, they had some outward forms of worship, but the essential principles of Christianity were not only not understood among them, but by many, never heard of. Some of the cardinal precepts of morality were disregarded, and actions plainly forbidden by the New Testament were often proclaimed by the clergy harmless and innocent, or at least foibles of but little account. Having no discipline, every man followed the bent of his own inclination. It was not uncommon for the rectors of parishes to be men of the loosest morals. The Baptist preachers were in almost every respect the reverse of the Established clergy. The Baptist preachers were without learning, without patronage, generally very poor, very plain in their dress, unrefined in their manners, and awkward in their address; all of which, by their enterprising zeal and unwearied perseverance, they either turned to advantage or prevented their ill effects. On the other hand, most of the ministers of the Establishment were men of classical and scientific education, patronized by men in power, connected with great families, supported by competent salaries, and put into office by the strong arm of civil power. Thus pampered and secure, the men of this order were rolling on the bed of luxury when the others began their extraordinary career. Their learning, riches, power, etc., seemed only to hasten their overthrow by producing an unguarded heedlessness, which is so often the prelude to calamity and downfall." [71]

---

[71] Semple, 25-26. Leland had already twenty years before Semple made substantially the same statement as to Baptist preachers. He speaks of "the rarity of mechanics and planters preaching such strange things," and adds in a note, " To this day (1790) there are not more than three or four Baptist ministers in Virginia, who have received the *diploma* of M. A., which is additional proof

The plain, everyday people, then, were not only irritated by social distinctions and wounded in the sensitive pocket nerve by burdensome church taxes, but they were shocked and disgusted by clerical immorality. Nor was this all. They saw their fellows and neighbors arrested and thrust like common malefactors into the county jails for the alleged crime of preaching the Gospel of peace, free to all men without tithe and without trammel of priestly contrivance. Looking at it in this way, they did well to be angry.

These illustrations of the Baptist propaganda and persecution and of their consequences have been thus fully set forth in order to show the passionate feeling of the Baptists themselves and the sympathy for them in the community at large in the latter part of 1774. This state of the public feeling led up to the resolution reached by the Baptists to make a direct attack on the Establishment as soon as possible. In 1773 an attempt to overthrow the Established Church would have been foolish and futile; in 1774 petitions to that end were subscribed to, Semple tells us, by "vast numbers readily and indeed eagerly."

It is well at this point, by way of review, to state briefly the relations of the Baptists and the legislature up to the middle of the year 1774. There do not appear to have been any petitions during 1771. Early in 1772, on Feb-

---

that the work has been of God, and not of man" (Writings, 105, and note, ibid.). Rev. R. B. C. Howell, in "Early Baptists in Virginia," an address delivered in 1856, nearly fifty years after Semple wrote, and nearly seventy years after Leland's "Virginia Chronicle," flatly contradicts the testimony of both these notable men as to this matter. What his authority is for so doing I know not; he gives none. See Publications of American Baptist Historical Society, 1857, p. 105 ff. Benedict says of these preachers: "A portion of the men under consideration possessed in a high degree the powers of imagination and invention to which many modern preachers of literary training can make but small pretensions. . . . Figures and metaphors were their favorite themes, and, by some means or others, they would make all things about them plain. As for parables, they would never leave one till they had made it go on all-fours." Benedict, Fifty Years, 96.

ruary 12, the Journal of the Burgesses shows that " A petition of several persons of the county of Lunenburg, whose
names are thereunto subscribed, was presented to the
House and read; setting forth, that the petitioners, being of
the society of Christians called Baptists, find themselves
restricted in the exercise of their religion, their teachers
imprisoned under various pretences, and the benefits of the
Toleration Act denied them, although they are willing to
conform to the true spirit of that act, and are loyal and
quiet subjects; and therefore, praying that they may be
treated with the same kind indulgence, in religious matters,
as Quakers, Presbyterians, and other Protestant dissenters
enjoy." [72]

Identical petitions are presented from Mecklenburg
county on February 22, and from Sussex on February 24;
and on this same day (Feb. 24) a like petition from Amelia
county adds that " If the Act of Toleration does not extend
to this colony, they are exposed to severe persecution; and
if it does extend hither, and the power of granting licenses
to teachers be lodged, as is supposed, in the General Court
alone, the petitioners must suffer considerable inconveniences, not only because that Court sits not oftener than
twice in the year, and then at a place far remote, but because
the said Court will admit a single meeting-house, and no
more, in one county, and that the petitioners are loyal and
quiet subjects, whose tenets in no wise affect the state; and
therefore praying a redress of their grievances, and that
Liberty of Conscience may be secured to them." [73]

On February 25, the Committee for Religion reported
that those petitions were reasonable and was ordered to
bring in a bill in accordance therewith. On the 27th of

---

[72] Journal, House of Burgesses, Feb. 12, 1772.
[73] Journal of Ho. of Burgesses, Fristoe, 73, says: " I knew the
General Court to refuse a license for a Baptist meeting-house in
the county of Richmond, because there was a Presbyterian meeting-house already in the county, although the act of Toleration
considered them distinct societies."

February this bill was reported, read a second time, and committed to the Committee for Religion.[74]

Another similar petition was presented from Caroline county on March 14, and was laid on the table.

On March 17, " Mr. Treasurer reported from Committee for Religion, to whom the bill for extending the benefit of the several Acts of Toleration to His Majesty's Protestant subjects in this Colony, dissenting from the Church of England, was committed." [75] The bill was ordered to be engrossed and to be " read the third time upon the first day of July next." But the House was prorogued on April 11, " to the 25th day of June next." The Journal shows no further entries until March 4, 1773. The house was prorogued again, March 13, by Lord Dunmore, and did not meet until May 5, 1774.

This Toleration Bill, proposed in February, 1772, was opposed by Baptists and by other dissenters as the next petition shows.

The year 1774 was a year of committees and correspondence, of petitions and expectation. The Virginia Committee of Correspondence was busily at work. The Virginia Burgesses had recommended the annual Congress of the Colonies, and its first meeting took place in September of this year in Philadelphia. Men's minds were excited in anticipation of coming change. Events were moving rapidly. The Baptists begun their general forward movement in the spring. At first it was defensive as before; it soon became offensive. It began with a petition for the improvement of their condition.

On May 12, 1774, " A petition of sundry persons of the community of Christians called Baptists, and other Protestant dissenters, whose names are thereunto subscribed, was presented to the House and read, setting forth that the toleration proposed by the bill, ordered at the last session of the General Assembly to be printed and published, not

---

[74] Cf. Journal of Burgesses.   [75] Ibid.

admitting public worship, except in the daytime, is inconsistent with the laws of England, as well as the practice and usage of the primitive churches, and even of the English Church itself; that the night season may sometimes be better spared by the petitioners from the necessary duties of their callings; and that they wish for no indulgences which may disturb the peace of Government; and therefore praying the House to take their case into consideration, and to grant them suitable redress." [76]

The House does not seem to have taken any action on the matter beyond referring it to the Committee for Religion. The petitioners, it is seen, were men busy at work during the daytime. This petition appears to be the joint work of individuals, Baptists and others. Perhaps it was shrewdly intended to accompany or precede the next petition noticed by the Assembly.

Four days later, on May 16, 1774, the House of Burgesses

" *Ordered*, that the Committee of Propositions and Grievances be discharged from proceeding upon the petition of sundry Baptist ministers, from different parts of this country, convened together in Loudon county at their Annual Association, which came certified to this Assembly, praying that an Act of Toleration may be made, giving the Petitioners and other Protestant dissenting Ministers, Liberty to preach in all proper Places, and at all Seasons, without Restraint. *Ordered*, that said Petition be referred to the consideration of the Committee for Religion; and that they do examine the Matter thereof, and report the same, with their Opinion thereon, to the House." [77]

This is an official petition from the Baptist representative body. It may have come from the Ketocton Association of the Regular Baptists held at Brent Town in 1774, although Brent Town was in Fauquier. The Separate

---

[76] Journal of House of Burgesses, May 12, 1774; also Meade, ii, 439.   [77] Journal of Burgesses, May 16, 1774.

Association for the Northern District was not held until the fourth Saturday in May, 1774, at Picket's Meeting-House in Fauquier county. The Separate Association for the Southern District [78] met on the second Saturday in May, as we have already seen,[79] and passed a resolution appointing fast days; but nothing is said of any petition to the Assembly.

It is a noteworthy conjunction of circumstances that on this same day, May 16, the Burgesses " *Ordered,* that Mr. Washington, Mr. Gray, Mr. Munford and Mr. Syme be added to the Committee for Religion." On the next day, May 17, Mr. Andrew Lewis, Mr. Macdowell and Mr. James Taylor were added to the same Committee. Jefferson had been added on May 9.

The Assembly was dissolved by Dunmore on May 26, and no legislative action was taken during the rest of the year.

With the advent of 1775, the political current began to run so strongly that all other interests were swept along with it. The Baptists, both from principle and from interest, were thorough republicans and ardent supporters of the revolutionary party. Speaking of it from the religious point of view, Semple says: "This was a very favorable season for the Baptists. Having been much ground under the British laws, or at least by the interpretation of them in Virginia, they were to a man favourable to any revolution by which they could obtain freedom of religion."[80] And Armitage, looking back across a hundred years at the situation, says: " . . . the Baptists demanded both (civil and religious liberty), and this accounts for the

---

[78] Semple does not note any petition from either of these associations to the General Assembly, nor do I find any note either of this petition or of the meeting of the Ketocton Association in Fristoe. Cf. Semple, 298, 301. Dr. C. F. James thinks this petition of the Ketocton Association may date back to 1771. Cf. *Religious Herald,* Jan. 12, 1899.

[79] See p. 16.   [80] Semple, 62.

desperation with which they threw themselves into the struggle, so that we have no record of so much as one thorough Baptist tory." [81] Thomas McClanahan, a preacher, raised a company of Baptists in Culpeper and took them into the army; John Gano and a number of other Baptist preachers are mentioned as being in active service; an increasing number of officers were or became Baptists as the war went on, and the rank and file was full of Baptist soldiers from the very beginning. Washington's testimony is given in his letter cited farther on. [82]

In May, 1775, both districts met as one association at Manakin-town or Dover meeting-house, Goochland county. Sixty churches were represented. The time was spent chiefly in prolonged and distressing debate on the question, " Is salvation by Christ made possible for every individual of the human race? " [83]

The petition " of sundry persons . . . . called Baptists, and other Protestant dissenters," already quoted, which had been presented to the Burgesses on May 12, 1774, was now presented to the Burgesses on June 13, 1775, and was ordered to lie upon the table. [84]

The districts met again as one association at Dupuy's meeting-house, Powhatan county in August, 1775, and proceeded vigorously to examine the things of this present world. " It seems that one great object of uniting the two districts at this time, was to strive together for the abolition of the hierarchy or Church establishment in Virginia. . . . . It was therefore resolved at this session to circulate petitions to the Virginia Convention or General Assembly, throughout the State, in order to obtain signatures. The

[81] Armitage, History of Baptists, 777.

[82] Life of Gano, pp. 94 ff.

This record should be made out and preserved. I would respectfully suggest to the learned and careful Editor of Semple's *History of the Baptists*, that he add to his services to Baptist history in particular and to Virginia history in general by drawing up a sketch of the Baptists from Virginia in the Revolutionary army.

[83] Semple, 55.   [84] Journal of Burgesses, June 13, 1775.

prayer of these was that the Church establishment should
be abolished and religion left to stand upon its own merits,
and that all religious societies should be protected in the
peaceable enjoyment of their own religious principles and
modes of worship. . . . They also determined to petition
the Assembly for leave to preach to the army." [85]   Jeremiah Walker, John Williams, and George Roberts were appointed a committee to wait on the convention. This matter is recorded in the Journal of the Convention as follows;
" An address from the Baptists in this Colony was presented to the Convention and read, setting forth—that however distinguished from their countrymen, by appelatives
and sentiments of a religious nature, they nevertheless consider themselves as members of the same community in respect to matters of a civil nature, and embarked in the
same common cause; that, alarmed at the oppression which
hangs over America, they had considered what part it
would be proper for them to take in the unhappy contest,
and had determined that in some cases it was lawful to go
to war, and that they ought to make a military resistance
against Great Britain, in her unjust invasion, tyrannical
oppressions, and repeated hostilities; that their brethren
were left at discretion to enlist, without incurring the cen-
sure of their religious community; and, under these circumstances many of them had enlisted as soldiers, and
many more were ready to do so, who had an earnest desire
their ministers should preach to them during the campaign;
that they had therefore appointed four of their brethren
to make application to this Convention for the liberty of
preaching to the troops at convenient times, without mo-
lestation and abuse, and praying the same may be granted
to them.

" *Resolved*, that it be an instruction to the commanding
officers of the regiments of troops to be raised, that they
permit the dissenting clergymen to celebrate divine wor-

---

[85] Semple, 62.

ship, and to preach to the soldiers, or exhort, from time to time, as the various operations of the military service may permit, for the ease of such scrupulous consciences as may not choose to attend divine services as celebrated by the chaplain." [86]   " This," says Dr. Hawks, " it is believed was the first step made towards placing the clergy, of all denominations, upon an equal footing in Virginia." [87]   It was the work of the Baptists alone, it is to be observed, and the step, though only a step, was a long one.

The occasion of this action of the Association was the ordinance of the Convention which met at " Richmond town " on July 17, 1775—" an Ordinance for raising and embodying a sufficient force for the defence and protection of this Colony." This provided for two regiments of regulars and also for sixteen regiments and battalions of minute-men in the sixteen districts into which the Colony was for that purpose divided. Each of these regiments and battalions was to have a chaplain to be appointed by the field-officers and captains, and when on duty the chaplain was to have a tent and be paid ten shillings a day—the pay of a major. [88]   Of course these positions would go to the clergy of the Establishment, ten shillings a day and all. The Baptists could hardly hope to get any of the appointments, nor does there seem to be any evidence that they tried to do so at this time. But to have their preachers appear before the men and preach under the authority of the Convention was a dear assertion of practical equality, and as new as it was dear. This petition then was no blind blow in the dark. But to the hopes of the preachers, the sequel must have been disappointing. " Jeremiah Walker and John Williams," says the candid Semple, " being appointed by this Association, went and preached to the soldiers, when encamped in the lower parts of Virginia, they,

---

[86] Journal of Convention of Aug. 16, 1775.
[87] Hawks, Protestant Episcopal Church of Virginia, 138.
[88] Hening, Statutes at Large, ix, 9 ff.

not meeting with much encouragement, declined it, after a short time." [89]

Though the interval of time be brief, it is a far cry from John Waller and John Schackleford, put in jail for preaching in March, 1774, to Jeremiah Walker and John Williams preaching to the soldiers under the authority of the Convention of the whole Colony in October or November of 1775.

This same ordinance classed together "all clergymen and dissenting ministers," along with the Committee of Safety and the president, professors, students, and scholars of William and Mary College, among the exempts from enlistment for military duty. [90] The usual exemption of "all Quakers, and the people called Menonites" from serving in the militia, is made in a separate section [91] as a matter of course and is without the significance attaching to this new classification. The ordinance also makes one provision which may have given the Baptists some influence in the matter of chaplains. It provides that the captains of the companies and the field-officers should be appointed by the committees of the various districts into which the Colony was divided. The field-officers and the captains appointed the chaplains. Thus it may have been possible for the Baptists to affect these appointments.

The Convention classed together the clergy and the dissenting preachers in a prohibition also. In the ordinance regulating the election of delegates to the Convention, it provided: "That all clergymen of the Church of England, and all dissenting ministers or teachers, should be incapable of being elected as a delegate, or sitting and voting in Convention." [92]

---

[89] Semple, 62.

[90] Hening, ix, 28. This section with fine courtesy exempts also "the members of His Majesty's Council."   [91] Hening, ibid., 34.

[92] Hening, ix, 57. This provision was distasteful to many Baptists, as the following extract from Leland shows: "If the office of a preacher were lucrative, there would be some propriety in

At the session at Richmond in December, 1775, the Convention provided for increasing the size of the two regiments and for raising six more regiments. In this ordinance it is directed that, in the great majority of counties, the captains should be appointed by the County Committees and the field-officers by the District Committees.[93] This would give the Baptists increased opportunity to exercise their influence, if they were disposed to do so.

The same ordinance makes another provision which shows how thoroughly the public needs and not abstract considerations of the rights of citizens were in the ascendant. "And be it further ordained, That hereafter no dissenting minister, who is not duly licensed by the general court, or the society to which he belongs, shall be exempted from bearing arms in the militia of this Colony." Apparently the number of preachers was being unduly increased by the exemption from service formerly declared. Greatness, too, has its penalties.

How desirous the State government was to conciliate all its citizens and to keep its forces in good condition is shown by the "Act for speedily recruiting the Virginia Regiments, etc.," passed two years later at the October session, 1777. One section provides: "And whereas there are within this commonwealth some religious societies, particularly Baptists and Methodists, the members of which may be averse to serving in the some companies or regiments with others, and under officers of different principles, though they would willingly engage in the defence of their country under the command of officers of their own religion: *Be it enacted*

---

his ineligibility; but as the office is not lucrative, the proscription is cruel. . . . In Virginia, their parsons are exempt from bearing arms. Though this is an indulgence that I feel, yet it is not consistent with my theory of politics; . . . an exemption from bearing arms is but a *legal indulgence*, but the ineligibility is constitutional proscription, and no legal reward is sufficient for a constitutional prohibition." (Writings, 122.) One is tempted to regret that Leland was not in the Convention.

[93] Hening, ibid., 75 ff.; ibid., 89.

" That such persons may raise companies, and if enough companies are raised, may form regiments having their own field-officers, chaplains, and so on." [94]

In the spring and summer of 1776, the Virginia Convention prepared and adopted the Declaration of Rights, with its immortal sixteenth section,[95] pronouncing religion henceforth free in Virginia (June 12, 1776), and also adopted the Constitution. In all this it does not appear that the Baptists as such took any direct part, though they doubtless did their duty as citizens, particularly at the polls.

The following remark by Fristoe makes it likely that they may have influenced the membership of this convention of 1776 as well as that of subsequent General Assemblies. Fristoe is speaking of the year 1776. " The business then was to unite, as an oppressed people, in using our influence and give our voice in electing members of the State Legislature—members favorable to religious liberty and the rights of conscience. Although the Baptists were not numerous, when there was anything near a division among the other inhabitants in a county, the Baptists, together with their influence, gave a caste to the scale, by which means many a worthy and useful member was lodged in the House of Assembly and answered a valuable purpose there." [96]

---

[94] Hening, ix, 348.

[95] This famous section is as follows: " A Declaration of Rights made by the representatives of the good people of Virginia, assembled in full and free Convention; which rights do pertain to them and to their posterity, as the basis and foundation of government. (Unanimously adopted June 12, 1776.)

" 16. That religion, or the duty which we owe to our Creator, and the manner of discharging it, can be directed only by reason and conviction, not by force or violence, and therefore all men are equally entitled to the free exercise of religion, according to the dictates of conscience; and that it is the mutual duty of all to practice Christian forbearance, love and charity towards each other."

Hening, ix, 109-112; cf. Bitting, Strawberry Association, p. 18.

[96] Fristoe, 90.

Eight days after the adoption of the Declaration of
Rights, " A petition of sundry persons of the Baptist
Church, in the County of Prince William, whose names are
thereunto subscribed, was presented to the Convention and
read; setting forth that at a time when this colony, with
others, is contending for the civil rights of mankind,
against the enslaving schemes of a powerful enemy, they
are persuaded the strictest unanimity is necessary, among
ourselves; and, that every remaining cause of division
may, if possible, be removed, they think it their duty to
petition for the following religious privileges, which they
have not yet been indulged with in this part of the world,
to wit: That they be allowed to worship God in their
own way, without interruption; that they be permitted to
maintain their own ministers and none others; that they be
married, buried, and the like, without paying the clergy of
other denominations; that, these things granted, they will
gladly unite with their brethren, and to the utmost of their
ability promote the common cause." The petition was referred to the Committee of Propositions and Grievances,
which was ordered to " inquire into the allegations thereof,
and report the same, with their opinion thereupon, to the
Convention." [97]

This petition was probably from the Regular Baptist
Church at Occoquon of which David Thomas was pastor,[98]
and may be considered the forerunner of the petitions to
the convention and of its consequent action at its next meeting in October as the General Assembly.

The next association had been appointed for Thompson's
meeting-house, Louisa county, on the second Saturday in
August, 1776. " They met accordingly," says Semple,
" and letters from 74 churches were received, bringing
mournful tidings of coldness and declension. This declen-

---

[97] Journal of Convention, under date.
[98] Semple; James, *Religious Herald*, Feb. 23, 1899.

sion is accounted for by some of the letters as arising from
too much concern in political matters, being about the
commencement of the Revolution. Others ascribed it to
their dissensions about principles, etc. Both doubtless had
their weight." This increase of nearly one-fifth in the
number of Separate churches since the May meeting of
1775, does not seem to an outsider to mark either coldness
or declension. There must have been between ninety and
one hundred Baptist congregations, organized and unor-
ganized, in existence at this time in Virginia. But it does
not appear that the Separates took any organic action in behalf of further religious liberty at this meeting of the Association, or at other meetings held in this same year and in
1777. Not indeed until 1778, as far as the records seem
to show, did the Association again petition the Legislature.
The dissensions among the Baptists themselves were sharp.
"This was an exceedingly sorrowful time," says Semple.

The Separate Association did not act, but the churches
as congregations or as individual members did act, if we
can attribute to the Baptists a share in the various petitions
presented in the fall of 1776. The Journal of the House of
Delegates often does not show from what denomination of
dissenters the petitions came; it generally does show if the
petition came from any representative body. The Baptists
were now numerous, probably the most numerous body of
dissenters in Virginia. They had in all probability already
adopted the custom, afterwards used by them, of sending
in petitions by counties so as to make the stronger impression on the legislature. It seems reasonable, therefore, to
give them credit for a share in these petitions not otherwise
accounted for. Accordingly in the pages following, such
petitions are mentioned as if emanating from Baptist
sources. This may be allowed the more readily because
from this time on the Baptists worked with others for religious freedom and against the Establishment; that is to
say, the Baptists were one element in a large and compli-

cated movement. The parts played by others in influencing legislative action will be set forth in due order.[99]

The first General Assembly of the State of Virginia met in Williamsburg on Monday, October 7, 1776. Among its early enactments was a bill which swept away all existing parliamentary laws restricting liberty of religious opinion and worship. This was done in part in response to the public demand as shown in petitions from many sources. The petitions probably or certainly from Baptist or partly Baptist sources are here given.

October 11, 1776. "A petition of sundry inhabitants of Prince Edward . . . that, without delay, all church establishments might be pulled down, and every tax upon conscience and private judgment abolished, and each individual left to rise or sink by his own merit and the general law of the land."—Referred to Committee for Religion.[100]

October 16, 1776. "A petition of dissenters . . . that having long groaned under the burthen of an ecclesiastical establishment, they pray that this, as well as every other yoke, may be broken, and that the oppressed may go free, that so, every religious denomination being on a level, animosities may cease," etc—Referred, etc.[101]

October 22, 1776. "Two petitions from dissenters from the Church of England in the counties of Albemarle, Amherst, and Buckingham . . . praying that every religious denomination may be put upon an equal footing."—Referred, etc.[102]

---

[99] Cf. Fristoe, p. 90-91.

These petitions exist in their original manuscript form in the State Library at Richmond, Virginia; but, owing to their chaotic condition, they are inaccessible. Not only the Baptists, but all those interested in the preservation of the sources of Virginia history should unite in an effort to secure an appropriation from the Virginia Legislature providing for the speedy cataloguing and publication of these valuable records. They would throw great light upon the genealogies as well as upon the social and political history of the State.

[100] Journal of House of Delegates, Oct. 11, 1776.
[101] Ibid., Oct. 16.   [102] Ibid., Oct. 22.

October 25, 1776. " Two petitions from dissenters . . .
praying that the ecclesiastical establishment may be suspended or laid aside."—Referred, etc.[103]

November 1, 1776. " Petition from dissenters . . . in
the counties of Albemarle and Amherst . . . praying that
every religious denomination may be put upon an equal
footing, independent of another."—Referred, etc.[104]

On November 9, 1776, it was " *Ordered*, That the Committee for Religion be discharged from proceeding on the
petitions of several religious societies, and that the same be
referred to the Committee of the whole House upon the
state of the country." [105]

On November 19, the Committee of the Whole reported
the following series of resolutions to the House: "*Resolved*,
As the opinion of this Committee, that all and every act or
statute, either of the parliament of England or of Great
Britain, by whatever title known or distinguished, which
renders criminal the maintaining any opinions in matters
of religion, forbearing to repair to church, or the exercising any mode of worship whatsoever, or which prescribes
punishment for the same, ought to be declared henceforth
of no validity or force within this Commonwealth.

. . . .

" *Resolved*, That so much of the petitions of the several
dissenters from the church established by law within this
Commonwealth, as desires an exemption from all taxes and
contributions whatever towards supporting the said church
and the ministers thereof, or towards the support of their
respective religious societies in any other way than themselves shall voluntarily agree is reasonable.

" *Resolved*, That though the maintaining any opinions in
matters of religion ought not to be restrained, yet that
public assemblies of societies for divine worship ought to
be regulated, and that proper provision should be made for

---

[103] Journal House of Delegates, Oct. 25, 1776.
[104] Ibid., Nov. 1.   [105] Ibid., Nov. 9.

continuing the succession of the clergy, and superintending their conduct.

"*Resolved*, That the several acts of Assembly, making provision for the support of the clergy, ought to be repealed, securing to the present incumbents all arrears of salary, and to the vestries a power of levying for performance of their contracts.

"*Resolved*, That a reservation ought to be made to the use of the said church, in all time coming, of the several tracts of glebe lands already purchased, the churches and chapels already built for the use of the several parishes, and of all plate belonging to or appropriated to the use of the said church, and all arrears of money or tobacco arising from former assessments; and that there should be reserved to such parishes as have received private donations, for the support of the said church and its ministers, the perpetual benefit of such donations."

The resolutions were adopted and it was "*Ordered*, That Mr. Starke, Mr. Treasurer (Robt. C. Nicholas), Mr. Jefferson, Mr. Bullitt, Mr. Tazewell, Mr. Mason, Mr. Madison, Mr. McDowell, Mr. Gordon, Mr. Zane, Mr. Fleming, Mr. Henry, Mr. Griffin, Mr. Lewis, Mr. Simpson, Mr. Read, and Mr. Johnson, do prepare and bring in a bill persuant to the said resolutions." [106] This was a notable committee.

On November 30, it was "*Resolved*, That the committee appointed to prepare and bring in a bill pursuant to the resolution of the whole House on the petitions of the several dissenters be discharged therefrom, except as to so much of the third resolution as relates to exempting the several dissenters from the established church from contributing to its support, so much of the fifth as saves all arrears of salary to incumbents, and empowers vestries to comply with their contracts, excepting also the sixth resolution; and that it be an instruction to the said committee to receive a clause, or clauses, to make provision for the

---

[106] Journal of House of Delegates, Nov. 19, 1776.

poor of the several parishes, to regulate the provision made
for the clergy, and to empower the several county courts
to appoint some of their members to take lists of tithables
where the same hath not been already done." [107]

On the same day " Mr. Starke, from the committee appointed, presented, according to order, a bill ' For exempting the different societies of dissenters from contributing
to the support and maintenance of the church as by law
established, and its ministers, and for other purposes therein mentioned '; which was read the first time, and ordered
to be read a second time." [108]   On December 2, the bill was
read a second time and ordered to be committed to a committee of the whole House.   On December 3 and 4 the bill
was considered and amended and ordered to be engrossed
and read a third time.   On December 5 the bill was passed
and carried to the Senate by Mr. Starke; and on December
9 the bill came back from the Senate with amendments; the
House adopted the amendments, and the bill became a
law. [109]

Mr. Jefferson thus records his recollection of this matter: " By the time of the Revolution, a majority of the
inhabitants had become dissenters from the Established
Church, but were still obliged to pay contributions to support the pastors of the minority.   This unrighteous com-
pulsion, to maintain teachers of what they deemed religious error, was grievously felt during the regal government, and without hope of relief.   But the first republican
legislature, which met in 1776, was crowded with petitions
to abolish this spiritual tyranny.   These brought on the
severest contests in which I have ever been engaged.   Our
great opponents were Mr. Pendleton and Robert Carter
Nicholas; honest men, but zealous churchmen.   The petitions were referred to the Committee of the whole House
on the state of the country; and after desperate contests in

---

[107] Journal House of Delegates, Nov. 30.   [108] Ibid.
[109] Journal of House, *passim.*

that Committee, almost daily from the eleventh of October
to the fifth of December, we prevailed so far only, as to
repeal the laws which rendered criminal the maintenance
of any religious opinions, the forbearance of repairing to
church, or the exercises of any mode of worship; and
further, to exempt dissenters from contributions to the support of the Established Church; and to suspend only until
the next session, levies on the members of that church for
the salaries of their own incumbents. For although the
majority of our citizens were dissenters, as has been observed, a majority of the Legislature were churchmen.
Among these, however, were some reasonable and liberal
men, who enabled us, on some points, to obtain feeble ma-
jorities. But our opponents carried, in the general resolutions of the committee of November 19, a declaration that
religious assemblies ought to be regulated, and that provision ought to be made for continuing the succession of the
clergy, and superintending their conduct. And in the bill
now passed was inserted an express reservation of the
question whether a general assessment should not be established by law on every one to the support of the pastor
of his choice; or whether all should be left to voluntary
contributions; and on this question, debated at every session from 1776 to 1779 (some of our dissenting allies, having now secured their particular object, going over to the
advocates of a general assessment), we could only obtain a
suspension from session to session until 1779, when the
question against a general assessment was finally carried,
and the establishment of the Anglican church entirely put
down." [110]

Mr. Jefferson minimizes the scope of this Act; [111] but in
fact, to sweep away all restrictions on religious opinion and
to exempt dissenters from all taxes for religious purposes,
was a victory as decisive as the passage of the religious

---

[110] Jefferson, Works, vol. i, pp. 31-32.
[111] For the law in full, see Hening, ix, 164.

section of the Declaration of Rights. It is true that the
Act purposely left open the question of a general assessment or of voluntary contribution for the support of the
clergy. But from the premises laid down in 1776 to the
conclusion reached in the great act of 1785, the process, if
slow, was logically inevitable, provided independence were
achieved.

As has already been stated,[112] the Baptists took no action
as a body, so far as any records that have survived seem
to show, at either session of the General Assembly in 1777,
though a meeting of one of the Associations was held in
April, 1777.

In May, 1778, a general Association was "holden" at
Anderson's meeting-house in Buckingham. Thirty-two
churches sent letters. "A committee was appointed to enquire whether any grievances existed in the civil laws that
were oppressive to the Baptists. In their reports, they
represent the marriage law as being partial and oppressive.
Upon which it was agreed to present to the next General
Assembly a memorial praying for a law affording equal
privileges to all ordained ministers of every denomination."[113] The Association met again this year in October
at Dupuy's meeting-house in Powhatan county, thirty-two
churches being represented. "A committee of seven members was appointed to take into consideration the civil
grievances of the Baptists and make report. (1) They reported . . . that should a general assessment take place,
that it would be injurious to the dissenters in general.
(2) That the clergy of the former established church suppose themselves to have the exclusive right of officiating
in marriages, which has subjected dissenters to great inconveniences. (3) They, therefore, recommend that two
persons be appointed to wait on the next General Assembly
and lay these grievances before them. Jeremiah Walker
and Elijah Craig (and in case of the failure of either), John

---

[112] See p. 42.   [113] Semple, 64.

Williams were appointed to attend the General Assembly." [114]

At this time it appears that the Association had lost hold on their members for some reason. Semple suggests "warm dissensions . . . combined with the ravages of war. From 60 and 70 churches which usually correspond, they had fallen to about 30 and 40. It seems that some had contracted unfavourable opinions of associations, and wished them to be laid aside." [115] Leland remarks: "Delegates from the churches assembled in associations once or twice in each year, but so much of the time was taken up in confiding what means had best be used to obtain and preserve equal liberty with other societies, that many of the churches were discouraged in sending delegates." [116]

Although this Committee was appointed in October, no petition is noted in the Journal of the House as from a Baptist source, except the petition of Jeremiah Walker, already cited,[117] asking for the refunding of his prison fee, and this was rejected. Whatever the source, however, the House had under consideration the matter of marriages, for on December 5, 1778, a bill "declaring marriages solemnized by dissenting ministers lawful" was presented and read the first time and was rejected two days later, December 7.[118] Evidently, only part of the story is told us by the existing records.

The Association met in May, 1779, in Goochland county. No account of this meeting is found.

At the spring session of the General Assembly in 1779, the committee for the revision of the laws submitted their report; and as this led to most important legislation, Mr. Jefferson's account of it is given here. He is speaking of what led up to the bill for religious freedom.

" Early, therefore, in the session of 1776, to which I returned, I moved and presented a bill for the revision of the

---

[114] Semple, 64.   [115] Ibid., 65.   [116] Leland, Writings, 113.
[117] See p. 19.   [118] Journal, December 7, 1778.

laws; which was passed on the twenty-fourth day of October, and on the fifth of November, Mr. Pendleton, Mr. Wythe, George Mason, Thomas L. Lee and myself were appointed a committee to execute the work. We agreed to meet in Fredericksburg to settle the plan of operation, and to distribute the work. We met there accordingly on the thirteenth of January, 1777. The first question was whether we should propose to abolish the whole existing system of laws and prepare a new and complete Institute, or preserve the general system, and only modify it to the present state of things. Mr. Pendleton, contrary to his usual disposition in favour of ancient things, was for the former proposition, in which he was joined by Mr. Lee. . . . . This last was the opinion of Mr. Wythe, Mr. Mason and myself. When we proceeded to the distribution of the work, Mr. Mason excused himself, as, being no lawyer, he felt himself unqualified for the work, and he resigned soon after. Mr. Lee excused himself on the same ground, and died indeed in a short time. The other two gentlemen, therefore, and myself divided the work among us. . . . . We were employed in this work from that time to February, 1779, when we met at Williamsburg, that is to say, Mr. Pendleton, Mr. Wythe and myself; and meeting day by day, we examined critically our several parts, sentence by sentence, scrutinizing and amending, until we had agreed on the whole. We then returned home, had fair copies made of our several parts, which were reported to the General Assembly, June 18, 1779, by Mr. Wythe and myself, Mr. Pendleton's residence being distant, and he having authorized us by letter to declare his approbation. We had in this work brought so much of the common law as it was thought necessary to alter, all the British statutes from *Magna Charta* to the present day, and all the laws of Virginia, from the establishment of our Legislature, in the 4th of Jae 1st (James I) to the present time, which we thought should be retained, within the compass of one hundred and twenty-seven bills, making a printed folio of ninety pages only. Some bills were taken out, occasionally, from time to time and passed; but the main body of the work was not entered upon by the Legislature, until after the general peace, 1785, when by the unwearied exertions of Mr. Madison, in opposition to the endless quibbles, chicaneries, perversions, vexations and delays of lawyers and demi-lawyers, most of the bills were passed by the Legislature, with little alteration. The bill for establishing religious freedom, the principles of which had, to a certain degree, been enacted before, I had drawn in all the latitude of reason and right. It still met with opposition; but with some mutilations in the preamble, it was finally passed." [119]

On June 4, 1779, Messrs. John Harvie, Mason, and Baker were ordered to prepare and bring in a bill " for religious freedom" and also a bill " for saving the property of the church heretofore by law established." The bills were read the first time on June 12, and on June 14 both bills were postponed " till the first day of August next " in order to get the sense of the people. Deep interest was shown in the bills, both for and against them.

At the meeting of the Association at Nottoway meeting-house, Amelia county, on the second Saturday of October, 1779, " the report by Jeremiah Walker, as delegate to the General Assembly, was highly gratifying upon which the following entry was unanimously agreed to be made:

"On consideration of the bill establishing religious freedom, agreed: That the said bill, in our opinion, puts religious freedom upon its proper basis; prescribes the just limits of the power of the State, with regard to religion, and properly guards against partiality towards any religious denomination; we, therefore, heartily approve of the same, and wish it may pass into a law. *Ordered,* That this our approbation of the said bill be transmitted to the public printers to be inserted in the Gazettes." [120]

---

[119] Jefferson, Works, i, pp. 34 ff.   [120] Semple, 65.

This additional extract from Semple shows the times: "It seems that many of the Baptists preachers, presuming upon a future sanction, had gone on to marry such people as applied for marriage. It was determined that a memorial should be sent from this Association requesting that all such marriages should be sanctioned by a law for that purpose. . . . . For a set of preachers to proceed to solemnize the rites of matrimony without any law to authorize them, might at first view appear incorrect and indeed censurable; but we are informed that they were advised to this measure by Mr. Patrick Henry, as being the most certain method of obtaining the law. It succeeded." [121]

The House Journal notes under October 25, 1779,[122] "a petition of the Baptist Association, setting forth that doubts have arisen whether marriages solemnized by dissenting ministers are lawful, and praying that an act may pass to declare such marriages lawful." On the same day a bill "concerning Religion" was presented by Mr. James Henry and read the first time, and was read again the next day, and sent to the committee of the whole House, for the following Tuesday, Nov. 2. A petition of sundry inhabitants of Amherst county was presented on Nov. 1, praying for the passage of the bill of the last Assembly "for establishing religious freedom."

On November 8, the Committee for Religion reported that the request of the Baptists as to marriages was reasonable, and the House ordered a suitable bill to be brought in.

November 10, 1779. "Divers of the freeholders and other free inhabitants of Amherst county," who afterwards describe themselves as "composed of Church of England men, Presbyterians, Baptists and Methodists," "unanimously and with one voice declare their hearty assent, concurrence, and approbation of the Act of January, 1779, declaring all church laws null, and the Act of Religious Free-

---

[121] Ibid., 65-66.
[122] Journal of House of Delegates, Oct. 25, 1779, and ff.

dom the true exposition of the Bill of Rights. Signed by a great number. Many for and against." [123]

On November 15, the bill concerning religion was put off " till first of March next," and Messrs. Mason, Henry, and General Nelson were ordered to bring in a bill " For saving and securing the property of the Church heretofore by law established," which bill was reported on November 26; and on November 29, the bill to amend an act concerning marriages was rejected.

On December 13, after being suspended since the October session of 1776, the bill for the support of the regular clergy was finally repealed by the House, and the Senate agreed. This repealing clause is as follows: " Be it enacted by the General Assembly—That so much of the act entitled—An act for the support of the clergy, and for the regular collecting and paying the parish levies, and of all and every other act or acts providing for the ministers, and authorizing the vestries to levy the same, shall be, and the same is hereby repealed." [124] This act severed the most important economic bond between Church and State in Virginia. It is not apparent that the Baptists had any immediately distinctive share in bringing about its passage.

The next Association met at Waller's meeting-house Spottsylvania county, May, 1780. No records. This Association seems to have petitioned the Assembly as appears under June 5, below.

The House Journal for 1780 notes: " May 12.—Petition from Amelia that marriages by dissenting ministers be declared lawful, also that vestries be dissolved.—Referred to Committee for Religion." [125] Many petitions for the dissolution of the vestries had been presented in preceding sessions. This is the first time that such a petition seems to have come from the Baptists.

---

[123] Cited from MS. Archives by Meade, vol. ii, 444-445. I give this for what it is worth. It seems inaccurate as it stands.
[124] Hening, x, 197.
[125] See House Journal under dates cited, here and hereafter.

Bishop Meade has the following entry concerning this petition:

" May 12, 1780.—Sundry inhabitants of Amelia pray that marriage licenses shall not continue to be directed, in the old form, to Episcopal ministers; that certain persons therefore doubted the validity of marriages by other than the Episcopal clergy; they pray that the ceremony ' without the use of the ring and the service ' may be declared lawful. Successful. It led to the bill legitimizing children of all such marriages by Dissenting ministers. The Baptist Association, at Sandy Creek, Charlotte, petition for the same. Also other Baptist Associations." [126]

One June 5, " a petition from the Society of people called Baptists was presented to the House expressing doubts as to the lawfulness of the marriages by their ministers, and praying that a law pass legalizing them. Referred to Committee for Religion."

On June 8, George Carrington from the Committee for Religion reported that they had had the two petitions under consideration, and that both were reasonable. The Committee was ordered to bring in bills accordingly.

On June 28 a bill " for the dissolving of Vestries and electing overseers of the poor " was ordered.

On July 4, a bill declaring " what shall be lawful marriage " was read once; it was read again on July 6, and was committed to the Committee on Propositions and Grievances. On July 7, this Committee reported the bill without amendment, whereupon the bill was engrossed, read a third time, and sent to the Senate. It did not become a law at this session.

On July 7 the bill for dissolving several vestries and electing overseers of the poor was read the third time and passed. It became a law [127] on July 11. [128]

---

[126] Meade, vol. ii, 445. This reference to the Association at Sandy Creek must be a mistake, for the May Association was at Waller's.

[127] Hening, x, 288.

[128] Overseers of the poor were substitutes for vestries in the " back counties," Rockbridge, Botetourt, Montgomery, Washington, Greenbrier, Augusta and Frederick.

The next Association was held at Sandy Creek, Charlotte county, October, 1780. Twenty-nine churches were represented. A committee from the Regular Baptists requested that a similar committee should be appointed by this Association to consider national grievances in conjunction with them. Reuben Ford, John Williams and E. Craig were appointed on the Committee. "The third Thursday in November following was appointed a day of fasting and prayer in consequence of the alarming and distressing times." [129]

At the fall meeting of the Legislature on November 8, 1780, a memorial and petition from the Baptist Association was presented, praying for a law for marriages by dissenting ministers and for the abolition of the existing vestry law. Referred.

On November 21, the Committee for Religion reported that they had considered the memorial of the Baptists asking for a marriage law for dissenting ministers, and that the request was reasonable. The Committee was ordered to prepare a bill accordingly. The Committee reported also in favor of dissolving the vestries. The resolution was tabled.

On December 2, the Committee for Religion reported a bill declaring " what shall be lawful marriage," and it was read once. The bill was read a second time on December 4, and re-committed. On December 15, the Committee reported the bill with amendments, and it was engrossed and read a third time. On December 18, the bill was passed and sent to the Senate, and became a law soon after.[130] The act provides: " For encouraging marriages and for removing doubts concerning the validity of marriages celebrated by ministers other than the Church of England, be it enacted by the General Assembly—That it shall and may be lawful for any minister of any society or congregation of Christians, and for the Society of Christians called

[129] Semple, 66.   [130] Hening, x, 361.

Quakers and Menonists, to celebrate the rites of matrimony, and to join together as man and wife, those who may apply to them agreeable to the rules and usage of the respective societies to which the parties to be married respectively belong, and such marriage, as well as those heretofore celebrated by dissenting ministers, shall be, and they are hereby, declared good and valid in law." The second section makes special provision for Quakers and Menonists. The third section fixes the marriage fee; and the fourth fixes the penalty for failure to return the marriage certificate to the Clerk of the County. The fifth section authorizes the County Courts to grant licenses to not more than four dissenting ministers of any one sect in any one county to join in matrimony persons within their county only. The act was to go into force on January 1, 1781. It is easy to imagine the relief brought by this act to many husbands and wives who were also fathers and mothers; and easy also to imagine the social heart-burnings and the bitter hatred against the Establishment that its delay had caused.

About May, 1781, Lord Cornwallis was marching through Virginia from the South, and consequently only sixteen churches met in Buckingham county in Association and quickly adjourned till October, 1782. For the same reason the General Assembly was a peripatetic body during its spring session and took no action on religious matters.

At the fall session, on November 22, 1781, "Sundry inhabitants of Prince Edward county prayed that all the old vestries may be dissolved by Act of Assembly and new ones elected by the body of the community at large. Dissenters to be equally competent with conformists to the post of vestrymen, and the sole proviso to be attachment to the present form of government." [181] This was referred to the next Assembly on December 22, and finally rejected.

---

[181] Meade, ii, 445; cf. Journal of Delegates, Nov. 22.

One of the Committee for Religion of this session was
Mr. Garrard. This is evidently the same man mentioned
by Semple in his history of the Ketocton Association: "In
this church arose James Garrard, late Governor of Kentucky. While in Virginia, he was distinguished by his fellow-citizens, and elected to the Assembly and to military
appointments." [132] He was a member also of the General
Assembly of 1785, and voted for the bill for Religious
Freedom.

The Association met next at Dover meeting-house,
Goochland county, in October, 1782. Thirty-two churches
were represented. "Finding it . . . considerably weari-
some to collect so many from such distant parts, and having already secured their most important civil rights, they
determined to hold only one more General Association, and
then dividing into districts, to form some plan to keep a
standing sentinel for political purposes. . . . . Jeremiah
Walker was appointed a delegate to attend the next General Assembly with a memorial and petitions against ecclesiastical oppression." [133] Walker was pastor of the Nottoway Church in Amelia (now Nottoway) county. He seems
for some reason to have had several of these petitions sent
up as coming from sundry inhabitants of that county.

This determination of the Association to "keep up a
standing sentinel for political purposes" shows clearly both
that the Baptists themselves were fully conscious that their
propaganda contained a powerful political element, and
that the public appreciated the fact also.

The Journal of the House of Delegates shows that on
November 22, 1782, the Committee for Religion reported
favorably on a part of a petition from Amelia county, asking the repeal of that part of the law defining lawful marriage which kept dissenting ministers from marrying people
beyond the limits of their own counties—and a bill to that
effect was ordered by the House; but reported unfavorably

---

[132] Semple, 315.   [133] Semple, 67.

on the part of the petition asking for the repeal also of the clause limiting the number of dissenting ministers who were to be licensed in each county to perform the marriage ceremony—and the House agreed to this part of the report also.

At the spring session of the Legislature in 1783, in response to a petition to authorize marriage by the civil authorities, the House, on May 30, ordered a bill to be brought in for " the relief of settlers on western waters." On June 25, this bill for " marriages in certain cases " was ordered to be engrossed and read a third time; it was passed and became a law on June 27.[134]   The bill provided that the county courts on the western waters might license " sober and discreet laymen " to perform the marriage ceremony in the absence of accessible ministers under certain conditions, and it legalized " all such marriages heretofore made."

On May 30 and 31, memorials of the Baptist Association praying for the repeal of the vestry law and for the repeal and amendment of parts of the marriage act were presented and referred.   On June 19, the bill " to amend the several acts concerning marriages " was deferred until October; on June 23 the bill concerning the vestries was likewise deferred until October.[135]

The General Association met for the last time at Dupuy's meeting-house, Powhatan county, on the second Saturday in October, 1783, with thirty-seven delegates present.   It was " *Resolved*, That our General or Annual Association cease, and that a General Committee be instituted, composed of not more than four delegates from each district Association, to meet annually to consider matters that may be for the good of the whole Society, and that the present Association be divided into four districts: Upper and Lower Districts, on each side of the James River. . . . .

---

[134] Hening, xi, 281.
[135] Journal of the House, under respective dates.

Reuben Ford and John Waller were appointed delegates to wait on the General Assembly with a memorial. Then dissolved." [136]

On November 6, 1783, " a petition of the ministers and messengers of the several Baptist churches" for repealing or amending existing vestry and marriage laws and asking for religious freedom were presented to the General Assembly and referred to the Committee for Religion. On November 8 a petition came up from Lunenburg county (probably from Episcopalians) asking for " a general and equal contribution for the support of the clergy"; a similar petition from Amherst county was presented on November 27; nothing was done. On November 15, the Committee reported on these petitions, and bills were ordered to be brought in revising the laws as to vestries and election of overseers of the poor and as to marriages. These bills were presented from the Committee for Religion on December 16. No action was taken at this session. [137]

On May 26, 1784, a memorial of the Baptist Association asking relief from the vestry and marriage laws and praying for perfect religious freedom was presented to the General Assembly and referred to the Committee for Religion of which Madison was a member. On June 8, the Committee reported, among other things, " that so much of the memorials from the United Clergy of the Presbyterian Church in Virginia, and the Baptist Association, as prays that the laws regulating the celebration of marriage, and relating to the constitution of vestries, may be altered; and that in general all legal distinctions in favor of any particular religious society may be abolished, is reasonable. That so much of the memorial from the clergy of the Protestant Episcopal Church, and the United Clergy of the Presbyterian Church in Virginia, as relates to an incorporation of their Societies is reasonable; and that a like incorporation ought to be extended to all other religious Societies within

---

[136] Semple, 68-69.   [137] Journal of the House, *loc. cit.*

this Commonwealth which may apply for the same."[138] Bills were ordered accordingly.

On June 25, the bill to incorporate the Protestant Episcopal Church was put off to the second Monday in November.[139]

The General Committee met for the first time on Saturday, October 9, 1784, with delegates from four Associations present. William Webber was appointed Moderator, and Reuben Ford, Clerk, and these positions they held, except for a few sessions, till the dissolution of the Committee in 1799. The important articles of their Constitution were: " 1. The General Committee shall be composed of delegates sent from all the district Associations that desire to correspond with each other. 2. No Association shall be represented in the general committee by more than four delegates. 3. The Committee thus composed shall consider all the political grievances of the whole Baptist society in Virginia, and all references from the district Associations respecting matters which concern the Baptist society at large. 4. No petition, memorial, or remonstrance shall be presented to the General Assembly from any association in connexion with the General Committee—all things of that kind shall originate with the General Committee."[140] We have here the usual machinery of political party organization with which our people have been familiar for many generations.

The Committee went vigorously to work. They drew up a memorial to the General Assembly for the repeal of the vestry law and for the modification of the marriage law, which they committed to their Clerk, Rev. Reuben Ford, for presentation; and they determined to oppose the proposed laws for a general assessment and for the incorporation of religious societies. The memorial was presented to

---

[138] Journal of the House, *loc. cit.*   [139] Journal of the House.

[140] Semple, 69-70. Compare this with the note from Thomas cited on p. 32.

the General Assembly, November 11, 1784, and was referred to the Committee for Religion, of which both Madison and Henry were now members. On November 17, the House ordered bills to be brought in regulating the laws as to marriage and the vestries; and ordered also a bill "to incorporate the clergy of the Protestant Episcopal Church." The House adopted the resolution "that acts ought to pass for the incorporation of all societies of the christian religion, which may apply for the same." Madison voted against it.[141]

The bill amending acts concerning marriage was read the third time on December 16, and sent to the Senate, and soon after became a law. It enacted "that it shall and may be lawful for any ordained minister of the Gospel in regular communion with any society of Christians, and every such minister is hereby authorized to celebrate the rites of matrimony according to the forms of the Church to which he belongs."[142] This put all ministers on the same footing before the law.

On December 28, the Senate passed the bill as amended incorporating the Protestant Episcopal Church.[143] By this law each vestry could hold property up to the value of a certain yearly income, could sue and be sued, like any other corporation, and could hold the glebe lands and the churches. This act soon after became an object of bitter attack.

For the present, however, the legislative subject that occupied the Baptists, and others, most engrossingly, was the bill brought in on December 2, read the second time the next day, and re-committed to the Committee of the Whole. It was entitled "A bill establishing a provision for the teachers of the Christian religion." It provided for a general assessment and that all persons should declare, when giving in their taxes, to what denomination they wished their assessments to go. If no such declaration were made,

---

[141] See Journal of House.　　[142] Hening, xi, 503.　　[143] Ibid., 532.

then the money so assessed was to go to encourage semi-
naries of learning in the respective counties. On December 24, by a vote of 45 to 38, the engrossed bill was postponed till the fourth Thursday in November, 1785; and it
was resolved that the bill and the ayes and noes thereon
should be printed and distributed throughout the State to
ascertain the sentiments of the people as to this legislation.
This was accordingly done, and resulted in wide-spread discussion and agitation.

At their next meeting, August 13, 1785, the Committee
heard with satisfaction from Reuben Ford of the amendments to the marriage law and with alarm of the engrossed
bill for a general assessment which had been deferred till
the next Assembly for the purpose of getting the sentiment
of the people on its provisions. The Committee promptly
" *Resolved*, That it be recommended to those counties which
have not yet prepared petitions to be presented to the General Assembly against the engrossed bill for the support of
the teachers of the Christian religion, to proceed thereon
as soon as possible; that it is believed to be repugnant to
the spirit of the Gospel for the Legislature thus to proceed
in matters of religion, that the holy Author of our religion
needs no such compulsive measures for the promotion of
His cause; that the Gospel wants not the feeble arm of man
for its support; that it has made, and will again, through
divine power, make its way against all opposition; and that
should the Legislature assume the right of taxing the
people for the support of the Gospel, it will be destructive
to religious liberty. *Therefore*, This Committee agrees
unanimously that it will be expedient to appoint a delegate
to wait on the General Assembly with a remonstrance and
petition against such assessment. Accordingly, the Rev.
Reuben Ford was appointed." This meeting of the Committee determined also to adopt for the Baptists the marriage ceremony as found in the Common Prayer book,
some omissions being made.[144]

---

[144] Semple, 71-72.

The terms of this resolution show that the Baptists had not waited for the meeting of their General Committee to begin to gird up their loins for the coming fight. The Committee "recommended to those counties which have not yet prepared petitions," runs the resolution, which means that many petitions were ready and waiting to swarm in upon the Assembly. The petitions enumerated below were not all from Baptists; but they are given as showing the state of public feeling.

The General Assembly met on October 17, 1785. Among the early bills passed was the "Act to provide for the poor of the several counties within this Commonwealth." This act provided for districts in the counties and for overseers of the poor to whom were to be transferred the powers of the churchwardens as to bastards, and also the powers and duties of the vestries.[145] This destroyed the civil power of the vestries, leaving them mere parts of the organization of the Protestant Episcopal Church.

On October 25, 1785, the Committee for Religion was appointed by the House.[146] On October 26, petitions against the bill making "provision for the teachers of the Christian religion," or the general assessment bill, as it was called, were presented from Cumberland and Rockingham; on October 27, similar petitions from Caroline, Buckingham, Henry, Pittsylvania, Nansemond, Bedford, Richmond, Campbell, Charlotte; October 28, from Accomac, Isle of Wight, Albemarle, Amherst; October 29, from Louisa; November 2, from Goochland, Westmoreland, Essex, Culpeper, Prince Edward, also the memorial and remonstrance of the Presbyterian Church in Virginia; November 3, from Fairfax, Orange, and also the "Memorial and Remonstrances of the General Committee of Baptists";[147]; November 5, from King and Queen; November 7, from Pittsylvania; November 9, from Mecklenburg,

---

[145] Hening, xii, 27.

[146] Journal of House under this date and so following.

[147] This noble paper, given by Semple, 435, and too long to print here, is by James Madison. Dr. Hawks says the bill for Religious

Amelia, Brunswick; November 10, from Middlesex; November 14, from Chesterfield, Fairfax; November 15, from Montgomery; November 17, Remonstrance of Baptist Association (Orange, September 17), also from Hanover, Princess Anne; November 18, from Amelia; November 28, from Henrico, Brunswick, Dinwiddie, Northumberland, Prince George, Powhatan, Richmond; November 29, from Spottsylvania, Botetourt, Fauquier, Southampton; December 1, from Lunenburg, Loudoun, Stafford, Henrico; December 10, from Washington, Amherst, Frederick, Halifax —in all, and not counting several petitions herein mentioned and others not mentioned, fifty-five hostile petitions from forty-eight different counties came within the space of a month and a half to remind the Legislators of the opinions of their constituents. Seven counties also sent petitions favorable to the bill, six of them in the list of counties given above and only one county, Surrey, sent a favorable petition and none other. Twenty-two counties out of seventy-one, less than one-third, sent no petitions.

In the presence of this exhibition of public sentiment, it is not surprising that the assessment bill was defeated; that on December 17, the bill for Religious Freedom passed to the Senate by a vote of seventy-four to twenty; that on January 16, 1786, the Senate amendments were agreed to; and that on January 19, 1786, signed by the Speaker of the House as an enrolled bill, the " Bill for establishing Religious Freedom " became the recognized law [148] of the land in Virginia, the first government in the world to establish and maintain the absolute divorce of Church and State, the greatest distinctive contribution of America to the sum of Western Christianized Civilization. [149]

Freedom was " preceded by a memorial from the pen of Mr. Madison, which is supposed to have led to the passage of the law." Prot. Ep. Ch. in Va., *passim.*

[148] Hening, xii, 84.

[149] It will be seen that the writer does not share the opinion that religious freedom had already been established in Rhode Island in 1644.

With the passage of the " Act of 1785," as it is generally known, the real struggle for religious freedom was over. Religious strife was not at an end, unhappily. But the struggle that followed was no longer that of the people ris-

---

This famous law is here given in the form in which it was reported to the General Assembly by Jefferson, Wythe, and Pendleton in 1779:

" Report of Committee of Revisors appointed by the General Assembly of Virginia in 1776.

Published by order of the General Assembly, June 1, 1784.

Dixon and Holt, Richmond, November, 1784. pp. 58-59.

CHAPTER LXXXII.

" BILL FOR ESTABLISHING RELIGIOUS FREEDOM.

SECTION I. Well aware that the opinions and beliefs of men depend not on their own will, but follow involuntarily the evidence proposed to their minds; that Almighty God hath created the mind free, and manifested his supreme will that it shall remain by making it altogether insusceptible of restraints; that all attempts to influence it by temporal punishments, or burthens, or by civil incapacitations, tend only to beget habits of hypocrisy and meanness, and are a departure from the plan of the holy author of religion, who being lord both of body and mind, yet chose not to propagate it by coercion on either, as was in his Almighty power to do, but to extend it by its influence on reason alone; that the impious presumption of legislators and rulers, civil as well as ecclesiastical, who being themselves but fallible and uninspired men, have assumed dominion over the faith of others, setting up their own opinions and modes of thinking as the only true and infallible, and as such endeavoring to impose them on others, hath established and maintained false religions over the greatest part of the world and through all times; that to compel a man to furnish contributions of money for the propagation of opinions which he disbelieves and abhors, is sinful and tyrannical; that even the forcing him to support this or that teacher of his own religious persuasion is depriving him of the comfortable liberty of giving his contributions to the particular pastor whose morals he would make his pattern, and whose powers he feels most persuasive to righteousness; and is withdrawing from the ministry those temporary rewards, which proceeding from an approbation of their personal conduct, are an additional incitement to earnest and unremitting labours for the instruction of mankind; that our civil rights have no dependence on our religious opinions, any more than on opinions in physics or geometry; that therefore the prescribing any citizen as unworthy the public confidence by laying upon him an incapacity of being called to offices of trust and

ing to demand their rights; it was rather of the kind which has so often verified the poet's caustic saying that " New Presbyter is but old Priest writ large."

The next General Committee, August 5, 1786, learned

---

emolument, unless he profess or renounce this or that religious opinion, is depriving him injuriously of those privileges and advantages to which, in common with his fellow-citizens, he has a natural right; that it tends also to corrupt the principles of that very religion it is meant to encourage, by bribing with a monopoly of worldly honors and emoluments those who will externally profess and conform to it; that though indeed those are criminal who do not withstand such temptations, yet neither are those innocent who lay the bait in their way; that the opinions of men are not the object of civil government, nor under its jurisdiction; that to suffer the civil magistrate to intrude his powers into the field of opinion and to restrain the profession or propagation of principles on supposition of their ill tendency is a dangerous fallacy, which at once destroys all religious liberty, because he being of course judge of that tendency will make his opinions the rule of judgment, and approve or condemn the sentiments of others only as they shall square with or differ from his own; that it is time enough for the rightful purposes of Civil Government for its officers to interfere when principles break out into overt acts against peace and good order; and, finally, that truth is great and will prevail if left to herself, that she is the proper and sufficient antagonist to error, and has nothing to fear from the conflict unless by human interposition disarmed of her natural weapons, free argument and debate; errors ceasing to be dangerous when it is permitted freely to contradict them.

SECTION II. We, the General Assembly of Virginia do enact that no man shall be compelled to frequent or support any religious worship, place or ministry whatsoever, nor shall be enforced, restrained, molested, or burthened in his body or goods, nor shall otherwise suffer, on account of his religious opinions or belief; but that all men shall be free to profess, and by argument to maintain, their opinions in matters of religion, and that the same shall in no wise diminish, enlarge or affect their civil capacities.

SECTION III. And though we well know that this Assembly, elected by the people for the ordinary purposes of legislation only, have no power to restrain the acts of succeeding Assemblies, constituted with powers equal to our own, and that, therefore, to declare this act irrevocable would be of no effect in law; yet we are free to declare, and do declare, that the rights hereby asserted are of the natural rights of mankind, and that if any act shall be hereafter passed to repeal the present or to narrow its operation, such act will be an infringement of natural right."

with pleasure " that the law for assessment did not pass;[150] but on the contrary, an act passed explaining the nature of religious liberty. This law, so much admired for the lucid manner in which it treats of and explains religious liberty, was drawn by the venerable Mr. Thomas Jefferson."[151]

The Baptists had now their full religious liberty. But the Committee were not satisfied. They were aggrieved that the Episcopalians should be incorporated and should hold possession of their glebes and churches. They, therefore, " *Resolved,* That petitions ought to be drawn and circulated in the different counties and presented to the next General Assembly, praying for a repeal of the incorporating act, and that the public property which is by that act vested in the Protestant Episcopal Church be sold, and the money applied to the public use, and that Reuben Ford and John Leland attend the next Assembly as agents in behalf of the General Committee."[152]

With the passage of the bill for Religious Freedom, as has already been said, the real struggle was over. But the momentum was too great; the impulse had to expend itself. The course it took was that commonly seen when a great popular party movement falls, so to speak, into the hands of those whom it has hitherto borne along. The part

---

[150] Semple rather claims for the Baptists the credit of defeating the General Assessment bill. " The Baptists, we believe, were the only sect who plainly remonstrated. Of some others, it is said that the laity and ministry were at variance upon the subject so as to paralyze their exertions either for or against the bill. These remarks, by the way, apply only to religious societies acting as such. Individuals of all sects and parties joined in the opposition " (pp. 72-73). Leland gives a somewhat different impression in his caustic remark on the subject: " When the time came, the Presbyterians, Baptists, Quakers, Methodists, Deists, and Covetous, made such an effort against the bill that it fell through " (Writings, p. 113). Leland wrote in 1789-1790; Semple wrote in 1809. " Deists and Covetous," quoth Leland. The economic principle never stops work.

[151] Semple, 72. It makes a singular impression on us to hear the active, eager, ever-young Jefferson called " the venerable "—as he was.   [152] Semple, 73.

played by the Baptists in the struggle for civil and religious liberty from 1774 to 1785 was admirable; the same cannot be said without qualification for their course from 1785 to 1802.

This part of our story can be told quickly, as there is no need to attempt to trace in it any phase of popular agitation.

At the session of 1786, the Assembly yielded to the pressure brought to bear on it, and repealed January 9, 1787, the Act incorporating the Protestant Episcopal Church but provided at the same time that each religious society should be secured in its property and authorized to regulate its own discipline.[153]

During all this period the law-making body regarded the Episcopal Church as the legal successor to the Established Church in the ownership of the property attached to it. Not so the Committee, as we shall see.

The fourth session of the General Committee, August 10, 1787, united the Separate and Regular Baptists under the name of the "United Baptist Churches of Christ in Virginia." They received the report from their legislative committee, Messrs. Ford and Leland, that the incorporation of the Protestant Episcopal Church as a religious society had been repealed, but that the law remained in force so far as the glebes and churches were concerned. "Whereupon, the question was put whether the General Committee viewed the glebes, etc., as public property; . . . by a majority of one they decided that they were. They did not, however, at this time send any memorial to the General Assembly."[154] Thus by a majority of one this body of preachers decided a grave question of law as to the ownership of the property of another denomination, and having once made the decision, they followed it with a pertinacity truly ecclesiastical.[155]

---

[153] Hening, xii, 266.   [154] Semple, 74.
[155] The legal aspects of this matter will be discussed in another connection.

"The next General Committee met at Williams's meeting-house, Goochland county, March 7, 1788. They considered whether the new federal constitution, which had now lately made its appearance in public, made sufficient provision for the secure enjoyment of religious liberty, on which it was agreed unanimously that, in the opinion of the General Committee, it did not. Whether a petition shall be offered to the next General Assembly, praying for the sale of the vacant glebes. After much deliberation on this subject, it was finally determined, that petitions should be presented to the next General Assembly, asking the sale of the vacant glebes as being public property; and, accordingly, four persons were chosen from the General Committee to present their memorial, viz., Eli Clay, Reuben Ford, John Waller, and John Willams." [156]

At the meeting in August, 1788, the Committee resolved "that the business should be entrusted to the care of Elders Leland, Waller, and Clay, to be left discretionary in them to present a memorial or not, as they may think best." [157] The memorial was presented.

The next meeting, held in Richmond, August 8, 1789, sent an address prepared by John Leland [158] to Washington, now President of the United States, as to the security of religious liberty under his administration. They received the following reply, worthy of the writer:

"To the General Committee representing the United Baptist Churches in Virginia: Gentlemen—I request that you will accept my best acknowledgements for your congratulation on my appointment to the first office in the nation. The kind manner in which you mention my past conduct equally claims the expression of my gratitude.

---

[156] Semple, 76-77. Semple adds a note: "The memorial was presented, and similar memorials and petitions continued to be presented to the legislature from the General Committee until 1799, when they gained their object." Bitting gives Mr. Clay's name as Eleazer.   [157] Semple, 78.   [158] Leland's Works, 52, note.

After we had by the smiles of Divine Providence or our exertions, obtained the object for which we contended, I retired at the conclusion of the war with the idea that my
country could have no further occasion for my services,
and with the intention of never entering again into public
life; but when the exigencies of my country seemed to re-
quire me once more to engage in public affairs, an honest
conviction of duty superseded my former resolution and
became my apology for deviating from the happy plan
which I had adopted.

" If I could have entertained the slightest apprehension
that the Constitution framed in the convention where I had
the honor to preside might possibly endanger the religious
rights of any ecclesiastical society, certainly I would never
have placed my signature to it; and if I could now con-
ceive that the General Government might ever be so administered as to render the liberty of conscience insecure,
I beg you will be persuaded that no one would be more
zealous than myself to establish effectual barriers against
the horrors of spiritual tyranny and every species of religious persecution.

" For you doubtless remember I have often expressed
my sentiments that every man conducting himself as a
good citizen, and being accountable to God alone for his
religious opinions, ought to be protected in worshiping the
Deity according to the dictates of his own conscience.

" While I recollect with satisfaction that the religious
society of which you are members have been throughout
America, uniformly and almost unanimously, the firm
friends of civil liberty, and the persevering promoters of
our glorious revolution, I cannot hesitate to believe that
they will be the faithful supporters of a free yet efficient
General Government. Under this pleasing expectation I
rejoice to assure them that they may rely upon my best
wishes and endeavors to advance their prosperity.

" In the meantime be assured, gentlemen, that I entertain

a proper sense of your fervent supplication to God for my temporal and eternal happiness.

"I am, gentlemen, your most obedient servant,

"George Washington." [159]

The minutes of the meeting of the Committee of May 10, 1790, state: "On a motion, it is desired that our Rev. Brethren who waited on the General Assembly last session, with a memorial and petition from the committee praying for the sale of the glebe lands, that are public property, and the opening of the churches for the different societies, do make their report. Accordingly they reported that, agreeable to their instructions, they waited on the Honorable Assembly; that the petition was presented to the house and received, but that the subject matter prayed for was not granted."

The Committee decided to present another memorial and petition to the next General Assembly and to recommend "that like petitions be presented from the different counties of the State." It was also "agreed to write to the Methodist Conference, to the Presbyterian Presbytery, and to President Smith, acquainting them with our purpose in the said petitions, and soliciting their assistance in obtaining subscribers." Committees were appointed to deliver these letters.

The Circular Letter to the Ministers of 1790 says: "We have agreed to make a vigorous exertion, for the sale of the glebes, and free occupation of the churches by all religious societies; and recommend it to you to do your endeavors, to get as many subscribers therefor as you can. And we also solicit contributions for the committee fund to defray the expenses of those who are appointed to wait on the Legislature with our memorial." [160]

With regard to the meeting of the Committee of May 14,

---

[159] Leland and Semple, *passim.* I give this valuable letter entire, as it is not found in the editions of Washington's writings by Sparks and Ford. [160] Quoted by Bitting, 23-24.

1791, Semple says: "The memorial against the glebes, etc., was the only business before them," and he also remarks that something "proved fatal to the rising prosperity of the General Committee. For from that session, it began to decline, and so continued until it was finally dissolved in the year 1799." [161]

The Committee evidently did not realize or believe that it was in any danger of declining as the following extract from the Circular Letter to the Minutes of 1791 shows: "We desire you to view us only as your political mouth, to speak in your cause to the State Legislature, to promote the interests of the Baptists at large, and endeavor the removal of every vestige of oppression. In the prosecution of this service, which we know was your original design in sending us here, we are determined to exert every nerve, till the heavy burdens are removed and the oppressed go free." [162]

Of the meeting at Tomahawk meeting-house, Chesterfield county, May 12, 1792, we are told: "The old question respecting the glebes and churches, as it was generally called, of course was taken up and fell into the usual channel." [163] Rippon's *Register* contains the following notice of this meeting: " . . . The Delegate who waited on the last General Assembly with a memorial and petition, informed the Committee, That agreeable to his appointment, he waited on the Assembly with said memorial; that it was received by the House, but that the prayer of the said petition was rejected. The Committee recommended that a lay member be appointed to wait on the Assembly with a memorial from the General Committee, remonstrating against those laws that have vested the glebe lands in the hands of the Vestry, and their successors, for the sole use of the Episcopal Church." [164]

---

[161] Semple, 81.   [162] Bitting, *loc. cit.*, 25.   [163] Semple, 84.
[164] Rippon's *Register*, vol. i, 1790-1793, pp. 534-5. It is interesting, though it may be purely accidental, that Semple writes upon this

The Minutes of the Meeting, May 15, 1792, add: "The
memorial being read and amended, was agreed to; and
brother Thomas Burford appointed to wait on the General
Assembly with the same, and the Rev. William Webber is
directed to give due notice in the public papers." [165]

This appointment of a layman to represent the General
Committee seems significant. The "great revival" was
over. It was not wise to press the clerical aspect of the
matter too far. Not only was the irreligious tendency of
the times to be taken into consideration, but the Virginia
Baptists as a class could not have felt in real need of more
liberty, however their committee of professional preachers
might feel about it. Thus the Rev. Isaac Backus, writing
from Middleborough, Massachusetts, July-October, 1789,
to Rippon's *Register*, says of the Virginia Episcopalians
"now their power is so gone that Episcopal worshipers
are but a small sect in that State and have no power to demand a farthing from any man for the maintenance of their
ministers; nor has any tax been gathered by force to support any denomination of Christians for three years past.
Equal Liberty of Conscience is established, as fully as words
can express it. O! when shall it be so in *New England?*
However, God is working wonders here." [166] And four
years later Rev. H. Toler writes to the *Register* from Westmoreland county, Virginia, April 5, 1793, "Liberty of conscience has been unlimited in this State ever since, or soon
after, the Declaration of American Independence; unless

occasion alone (p. 84), "the glebes and churches." Otherwise he
invariably writes, as far as I have noticed, "the glebes, etc." The
Baptists were not trying only to sell the glebes but also to open
by law to other denominations the churches that had belonged to
the Establishment. There seems to be nothing to show that the
Baptists wanted either to sell or to destroy the churches themselves. That was, however, in many cases the result of their action,
and Semple was writing at a time when that result was plainly and
painfully evident.

[165] Quoted by Bitting, *loc. cit.*, 26.
[166] Rippon's *Register, loc. cit.*, 94.

the case of the glebes, mentioned in the Minutes of the General Committee, be an exception." [167]

" The General Committee," Semple tells us, " continued to be holden at the usual time of the year, at the following places (which are enumerated down to) 1799 at Waller's meeting-house, Spottsylvania county, where they agreed to dissolve. During this period, an unreasonable jealousy of their exercising too much power was often manifested both by associations and individuals. This added to some other courses, produced a gradual declension in the attendance of members as well as a nerveless languor in the transaction of business. The remonstrance respecting glebes, etc., was the only business which excited no jealousies, and that was the only matter which was ever completed after the year 1792." [168]

The letter from the Dover Association to Rippon's *Register* under date of October, 1800, states that the Committee, while holding their meeting in Spottsylvania in May, 1799, heard that the prayer of their memorial to the last General Assembly as to glebe lands was granted, and adds: " The Committee, therefore, having secured their object, do not think it expedient to exist any longer. But sufficient praise is not easily to be given to them for their perseverance." [169]

The General Assembly at their meeting in 1798, took up, finally, this matter of the glebes and disposed of it as to the right of ownership in them. On January 24, 1799, an act was passed " to declare the construction of the bill of rights and constitution concerning religion." This act recites that various preceding acts, of 1776, 1779, 1784, etc., " do admit the Church established under the regal government to have continued so, subsequently to the constitution; have bestowed property upon that Church; have asserted a legislative right to establish any religious sect, and have

---

[167] Rippon's *Register, loc. cit.,* 543.   [168] Semple, 85.
[169] Rippon's *Register,* vol. 1801-1802, p. 789.

incorporated religious sects, all of which is inconsistent with the principles of the constitution and of religious freedom and manifestly tends to the establishment of a national Church "; it then repeals all these laws.[170] This caused all the property in any way held by Episcopal Church organization to revert to the public fisc, unless for some special reason retained.

Affairs remained in this condition until the session of 1801, when the Legislature returned to the charge and on January 12, 1802, passed a bill directing the overseers of the poor to sell the glebes for the benefit of the public. The preamble to this bill sets forth that " the General Assembly on the twenty-fourth day of January, 1799, by their act of that date, repealed all the laws relative to the late Protestant Episcopal Church, and declared a true exposition of the principles of the bill of rights and constitution respecting the same to be contained in the act entitled ' An act for establishing religious freedom ' (Jefferson's law of 1785); thereby recognizing the principle that all property formerly belonging to the said Church, of every description, devolved on the good people of this Commonwealth on the dissolution of the British government here in the same degree in which the right and interest of the said Church was therein derived from them; and that although the General Assembly had the right to authorize the sale of all such property indiscriminately, yet being desirous to reconcile all the good people of this Commonwealth, it was deemed inexpedient at that time to disturb the possession of the present incumbents." The law then enacted that in any county where any glebe was or should become vacant, the overseers of the poor should have full power to sell the same. The proceeds were to be appropriated to the poor of the parish, or to any other object which a majority of freeholders and housekeepers in the parish might by writing direct, provided that nothing should authorize an ap-

---

[170] Code of Virginia, cf. Churches.

propriation of it " to any *religious* purpose whatever." The
church buildings, with the property contained in them, and
the churchyards were not to be sold under the law, neither
were any private donations made before the year 1777 to
be sold, if there were any person in being entitled to hold
property under the original donor.   Gifts of any kind made
after the year 1777 were left untouched.[171]

" The warfare," says Dr. Hawks sententiously, " the warfare begun by the Baptists seven-and-twenty years before,
was now finished." [172]

This selling of the Church property was not the work of
the Baptists alone by any means; but both from their numbers and from the continuity of their organized attack,
they seem to have been the dominant influence.   Year after
year from 1786 to 1799, with the possible exception of the
year 1787, memorials went in to the General Assembly
from the General Committee, demanding the sale of the
glebe lands as an act of justice and of public right.   During this same period the members of the General Assembly
who were themselves Baptists or of Baptist sympathies in
the matter must have steadily increased.   The " great revival" of 1785 to 1792 was going on.   A letter in 1789
from Dr. ——, in New York to Rippon's *Register* says:
" I have the most credible information that nearly one-half
the inhabitants of both Virginia and North Carolina are
Baptists, or inclining to those sentiments now."   And a
letter from Baltimore a few months later, February 4, 1790,
adds: " A few months since I received a letter from one
of the ministers in said State (Virginia), giving an account
of between four and five thousand persons added to one
association in less than fifteen months' time." [173]   These estimates are doubtless exaggerations of fact, but probably
not of public belief about the fact.   Semple writes of this

---

[171] Code of Virginia, Churches.
[172] Hawks, Protestant Episcopal Church in Virginia, 233.
[173] Rippon's *Register*, vol. 1790-93, 100-101.

revival: "It continued spreading until about 1791 or 1792. Thousands were converted and baptized, besides many who joined the Methodists and Presbyterians. The Protestant Episcopalians, although much dejected by the loss of the Establishment, had nevertheless continued their public worship, and were attended by respectable congregations. But after this revival, their society fell fast into dissolution." [174] Under these conditions, it is not surprising that the laws of 1799 and 1802 should have been passed, nor that the law of 1802 should have been executed with a harsh disregard of minor rights. The axe was laid to the root.

Whatever may be our opinion of the spirit of this sectarian pursuit of another sect, we cannot help feeling that the logic of the event was worked out with a just completeness rare in history. So far as the Baptists were concerned, the Established Church from 1768 to 1774 had taught "instructions which being taught returned to plague" her successor, the Protestant Episcopal Church, from 1784 to 1802. During all those years, the Baptists followed with passionate eagerness the ideal of religious freedom to its logical consequence of absolute separation of Church and State. In the process they had a large share, and for the result they deserve immense credit.

.   .   .   .

The spread of Baptist and Presbyterian doctrine in Virginia during the years immediately preceding and including the Revolution, with the religious and political consequences ensuing, seems almost a repetition, due allowance being made, of what took place in England during the first half of the seventeenth century. Of Virginia too it might be said as has been said of the mother country: "Virginia became the land of a book, and that book the Bible."

In fact, the Baptists represent in Virginia history be-

---

[174] Semple, 38.

lated politico-religious Puritanism—not imported, not the
Puritanism of England nor of New England, but native,
genuine, and characteristic.[175] The Quakers, suspected
and feared when they first came into the Colony, never ac-
quired extended nor permanent influence over the population. The average Virginian has loved and still loves too
much expression and not repression. He looked upon the
idea of non-resistance, passive, active, or in any other mood
and tense as a reflection upon his manhood. The nobler
aspects of Quakerism were for him largely obscured by
their peculiar sectarian conditions. The handful of General Baptists in the southeastern corner of the Colony remained for fifty years a handful, almost unknown and without influence. The mass of the Presbyterians were at first
immigrants of the sturdy Scotch-Irish stock; they brought
their opinions with them, ready formulated in a distinctive
creed. The Methodists were Puritan in the original sense
of the word; but they remained with and in the State
Church all during the Revolution, not separating from it
until about twelve months before the passage of the Act
for Religious Freedom.

Puritanism, then, even during the Commonwealth time,
had never made itself a home in Virginia as in other colonies, Maryland, for example.[176] Virginia had been and
remained in her social, religious, and political life the most
purely English of all the colonies. Conservative because
of her widely scattered agricultural and plantation life, rendered still more conservative by the inevitable conditions
accompanying the slavery of an alien race, Virginia felt, but

---

[175] They represent also the popular resistance to Virginia semi-
feudalism, a feudalism at once an incipiency and a survival. Mr.
John Morley, speaking (in his *Oliver Cromwell*, p. 23) of John Pym,
says: " He was a Puritan in the widest sense of that word of many
shades; that is to say, in the expression of one who came later,
' he thought it part of a man's religion to see that his country
be well governed,' and by good government he meant the rule of
righteousness both in civil and in sacred things."

[176] Fiske, Old Virginia and her Neighbors, i, 301-318; ii, 17-18.

did not yield to the impulse of either Quaker or Presbyterian. Slowly she ripened to the harvest. As in England, not until the social, religious, and economic conditions were favorable, did the political aspiration of the race for freedom have free vent; and then, as in England again, Teutonic individualism appeared rampant. Constrained at once and encouraged by the march of political events, this individualism gave itself free reign in religion, and, as in England just before the downfall of divine Monarchy, a kind of religious anarchy spread in Virginia, a tremendous revolutionary impulse which rapidly consolidated under the Baptist form of church organization with the Bible as the sole standard of faith.

It is this aspect which makes, in part, that early Baptist movement in Virginia of such exceeding interest to the student of history and to the lover of freedom. The people themselves were of very pure English breed, and they belonged to the yeomanry of the country. The movement was a movement " of the people, by the people, for the people "; and its aim was freedom.

In this brief sketch we have seen the rapid dissemination of Baptist religious principles under the operation of the religious, social, and economic conditions of the period just prior to the outbreak of the American Revolution; we have seen the great impetus given to those principles and the alliance formed with them by the patriotic principles of political freedom—the mainspring of the succeeding contest; we have seen how, under these influences, the Baptist organization, perhaps unconsciously, adopted the political form, and, thus armed, thrust pitilessly against the opposing religious organization until it helped to strike it down; we have seen that, though another church was fiercely followed, no individual as such was attacked or robbed of his rights; and we have seen that, at the end of the struggle, the Baptists had been largely instrumental in putting Virginia in the lead of the civilized nations in the assertion of the absolute freedom of religious faith from civil control.

This was a great achievement, a thing new in the history of the world. And it is a record of which any denomination and any people may be proud, this record of the plain, every-day people of our land. For the plain people knew then, as they know now, in government as in morals, that it is the truth that shall make us free.

BIBLIOGRAPHY.

Armitage, Thomas.   History of the Baptists.   N. Y., 1887. 1 vol.

Asplund, John.   The Annual Register of the Baptist Denomination in North America to November 1, 1790.

Bailey, G. S.   The Trials and Victories of Religious Liberty in America.   1776.   A Centennial Memorial, 1876. American Baptist Publication Society, Phila.

Beale, G. W.   Semple's History of the Baptists in Virginia. Revised and Extended.   Richmond, Virginia, 1894.

Benedict, David.   History of the Baptist Denomination. Boston Massachusetts, 1813.   2 vols.

—— Fifty Years among the Baptists.   New York, 1860. 1 vol.

Bitting, C. C.   Religious Liberty and the Baptists.   Bible and Publication Society, Philadelphia.

—— Notes on the History of the Strawberry Baptist Association of Virginia for One Hundred Years—from 1776 to 1876.   Published by the Association, 1879.

Bruce, Philip A.   Economic History of Virginia in XVII Century.   New York, 1896.   2 vols.

Campbell, C.   History of Virginia.   Philadelphia, 1860.

Curry, J. L. M.   Struggles and Triumphs of Virginia Baptists.   The Bible and Publication Society, Phila., 1873.

—— Establishment   and   Disestablishment.   American Baptist Publication Society, Philadelphia, 1889.

Edwards, Morgan.   Materials towards History of the Baptists.   (History of Virginia Baptists ends 1772.)   1 vol.

Fiske, John.   Old Virginia and Her Neighbors.   Boston, 1897.   2 vols.

Foote, W. H.   Sketches of Virginia.   Series I.   Philadelphia, 1850.   1 vol.

Fristoe, William.   History of the Ketocton Baptist Association.   Staunton, Virginia, 1808.   1 vol.

Gano, John.   Life of Gano.   New York, 1806.   1 vol.

Hawks, F. L.   Protestant Episcopal Church in Virginia. New York, 1836.

Henry, W. W.   Life of Patrick Henry.   New York. 2 vols.

Hurst, J. F.   Literature of Theology.   New York, 1896. 1 vol.

Howell, R. B. C.   Early Baptists of Virginia.   Publications American Baptist Historical Society.   Philadelphia, 1857.

James, C. F.   Documentary History of the Struggle for Religious Liberty in Virginia.   *Religious Herald*, Richmond, Va., December 8, 1898, and following numbers.

Jefferson, Thomas.   Writings of.   Washington, D. C. 9 vols.

Leland, John.   Writings (ed. by Miss L. F. Green).   New York, 1845.   1 vol.

McIlwaine, H. R.   Struggle for Religious Toleration in Virginia.   J. H. U. Studies in Hist. and Polit. Science, 1894.

Mason, George.   Life of, by Kate Mason Rowland.

Meade, William.   Old Churches and Families of Virginia. Philadelphia, 1885.   2 vols.

Rippon, John.   Baptist Annual Register.   London.   4 vols. 1790-1793, 1794-1797, 1798-1801, 1801-1802.

Semple, R. B.   History of the Rise and Progress of the Baptists in Virginia.   Richmond, Virginia, 1810. 1 vol.

Taylor, James B.   Virginia Baptist Ministers.   Series I., 3rd ed., New York, 1860, 1 vol.; Series II, New York, 1860.   1 vol.

Thomas, David. The Virginia Baptist, Baltimore, 1774.
    1 vol.

Virginia Almanac for 1776, 1778, 1779. By David Ritten-
    house, Williamsburg, Virginia.

Virginia, House of Burgesses, Journals of.

Virginia Conventions, Journals of, 1775, 1776.

Virginia, General Assembly of, Journals of.

Virginia, Statutes at Large. W. W. Hening. 13 vols.

Virginia, Code of.

Washington, George. Writings of.

Watson, Elkanah. Men and Times of the Revolution.
    2 ed., New York, 1856.

INDEX

A

Adams, *Prof.* Herbert B., dedication to, 9; on "The Church and Popular Education," 393-476; 402 (note), 426, 439 (note), 444, 459, 467 (note).

Adams, *Dr.* T. S., public lecture, 450; on Taxation in Md., 13-75.

Administrators, tax on commissions of, 19, 21, 22, 34, 62-63.

America, causes of colonization, 261.

Ames, Adelbert, governor of Mississippi, 192.

Andrews, *Dr.* C. M., public lectures, 439-440.

Appeal Tax Court of Maryland, 34-39.

Armstrong, R. A., quoted, 464.

Arnold, Matthew, cited, 495.

B

Backus, *Rev.* Isaac, quoted, 563.

Ball, W. D., popular lectures, 456-460, 461-463.

Baltimore, predominance in Maryland, 14-15; population, 16; taxation, 29, 34-38, 40, 41, 50, 63, 71, 72. *See also* "Maryland"; educational work of churches, 430-467; founding of, 430.

Baltimore and Ohio R. R., dividends to state (Maryland) cease, 20.

Banks, opposition to, in Kansas, 127; in Iowa, 359-360, 371-373, 377-378, 379-382; taxation in Maryland, 61; in North Carolina, 100, 113; in Kansas, 149 (note); in Mississippi, 198, 199; in Georgia, 221, 239-240.

Baptists, educational work of churches, 441-443; Struggle for Religious Freedom in Virginia, 485-572; connection of struggles for religious and political freedom, 485; three branches, 486-488; constitution of a church, 490 (note), 513 (note); proselyting zeal, 489-492; revivals, 492-494; opposition of the ignorant classes, 495-497; arrests on peace warrants and punishments, 497-502; seat of persecution, 503; attitude of the Established Church, 503-504; petitions to General Assembly, 504-505; greatest period of persecution, 505; first session of association of "Separates," 505; growth of church, 505-506; causes of growth, 506-509; questions of dress, 510; grounds of opposition to the Established Church, 510-513, 516-520; numbers of, 514-518; petitions for toleration, 520-523; Revolutionary War, 526-528; first steps towards equality of clergy, 526-530; "sixteenth section," 530; petitions for religious freedom, 531-534; dissenters exempted from tithes, 534-538; salaries of clergy, 543; dissolution of vestries, 543, 544; civil power of vestries destroyed, 553-554; marriages by dissenting ministers, 538, 539, 542, 543, 544, 545-546, 547, 548, 549, 551; formation of General Committee, 548-549; union of "Regulars" and "Separates," 555; act of 1785 ending struggle for religious freedom, 555-556; subsequent career less praiseworthy, 557-558; act incorporating Protestant Episcopal Church repealed, 558; disposal of glebe lands, 558-566; Baptists were Puritans, 567-570; bibliography, 570-572.

Miner's Book of Dubuque, incorporated, 359.

Mississippi, economic characteristics, 177-179; state debt, 181-182, 191; formation of territory, 184; public education, 197, 205, 215. Taxation, 177-215; county, unit of taxation, 179; receipts and expenditures, 180, 182-183; back-tax collections, 181; territorial period, 184-187; period of ante-bellum statehood, 187-189; war period, 189-191; reconstruction period, 190-193; modern period of fiscal reform, 193-195; present rates, 178, 195. General property, 186-187, 195, 196-206; nature, 196; " Madison Law," 196 (note); maximum limit, 197; exemptions, 190, 197-198; assessment, 198-199; banks, 198, 199; railroads, 190, 200, 208, 211; collection, 200-201; escape of personalty, 202; rigidity and complexity, 204-206. Corporation taxation, not distinct from general property, 202-203, 214. Privilege-license, 177, 180, 181, 206-212, 214; displaces fee system, 181; varieties, 206-210; partial exemptions of Confederate veterans, 210; defects, 211-212. Poll tax, 179, 186, 195, 212-213; importance, 212-213; influence on suffrage, 213. Inheritance tax, 191; possible reforms in taxation, 213-215; bibliography, 215.

Morgan, Jas. M., quoted, 370.

" Moses and Aaron of New Haven," 298.

Mortgages, in Maryland, 34, 43, 64, 73-75; taxation in Kansas, 160, 168.

Mount Calvary, educational work, 435-438.

Murray, *Dr.* David, 403.

N

Negro, attitude of Iowa: convention of 1844, 356-358; effect of Missis-

sippi poll tax upon suffrage, 213; convention of 1857, 382-387.

New Haven, settlement, 296-297.

O

Official commissions, taxation of (Maryland), 64.

Oort, *Dr.,* on Biblical education, 464.

Ordinance of 1787, 405; denounced, 363-364.

" Organic Law " of Iowa, 347-350.

" Oyster Fund " (Maryland), 17.

P

Palatinate, colony of Maryland, 299 (note).

Parkhurst, *Dr.* Chas. H., public lecture, 463.

" Parsons' Cause " (Virginia), 511.

People's Church (St. Paul), practical activities, 423.

Pilgrim Church (Worcester), practical activities, 421.

Plymouth, colony of, 292; Company dissolved, 292.

Plymouth Church (Milwaukee), practical activities, 422-423.

Plymouth Church (Salina), practical activities, 423.

Poll tax. *See* " Georgia," " Kansas," " Maryland " " Mississippi," and " North Carolina."

Poor's Manual, quoted on earnings of railroads, 53-54.

Presbyterian churches in educational work, 438-439.

Princeton University, origin, 403-404.

Privilege-license taxes. *See* " Mississippi."

Privy Council, relations with American colonies, 309, 312, 314, 315.

Professions, taxation in Georgia, 238.

Property, general and personal. *See* " Georgia," " Kansas," " Maryland," " Mississippi," and " North Carolina."

Protests, tax on in Maryland, 63-64.